Drastic Dislocations

New and Selected Poems

Previous Books by Barry Wallenstein

Poetry

Tony's World, Delhi, NY, Birch Brook Press, 2009
The Tony Poems, Canada, Ottawa, Lyric Editions, 2001
    [Illustrated by Chan Ky-Yut]
A Measure of Conduct, Detroit, MI, Ridgeway Press, 1999
The Short Life of the Five Minute Dancer, Detroit, MI, Ridgeway
    Press, 1993
Love and Crush, NY, Persea Books, 1991
Roller Coaster Kid, NY, T.Y. Crowell, 1982
Beast Is A Wolf With Brown Fire, Brockport, NY, BOA Editions, 1977

Critical Study

Visions and Revisions: The Poet's Practice, [edited with Bob Burr]
    Peterborough, Ontario, Canada, Broadview Press, 2002

Anthologies

For Enid with Love: A Festschrift, editor; NYQ Books, NY, 2010
Years of Protest: A Collection of American Writings of the 1930's,
    [edited with Jack Salzman], Pegasus, NY, 1967

Recordings of Poetry with Music

Euphoria Ripens, Cadence Jazz Records, CJR 1210, 2008
Pandemonium, Cadence Jazz Records, CJR 1194, 2005
Tony's Blues, Cadence Jazz Records, CJR 1124, 2001
In Case You Missed It, SkyBlue Records, CD 106, 1995
Taking Off, AK-BA Records, 1040,
    [Reissued by Bleu Regard, CT 1950, 1995] 1982
Beast Is, AK-BA Records, 1020, 1978

Drastic Dislocations

New and Selected Poems

Barry Wallenstein

The New York Quarterly Foundation, Inc.
New York, New York

NYQ Books™ is an imprint of The New York Quarterly Foundation, Inc.

The New York Quarterly Foundation, Inc.
P. O. Box 2015
Old Chelsea Station
New York, NY 10113

www.nyqbooks.org

Copyright © 2012 by Barry Wallenstein

All rights reserved. No part of this book may be used or reproduced in any manner whatsoever without written permission of the author.

First Edition

Set in New Baskerville

Layout and Design by Raymond P. Hammond
Cover Design by Carol McDonald | www.barefoot-creations.com

Library of Congress Control Number: 2011937870

ISBN: 978-1-935520-43-6

Drastic Dislocations

New and Selected Poems

This book is for Lorna, Daniel and Jessica.

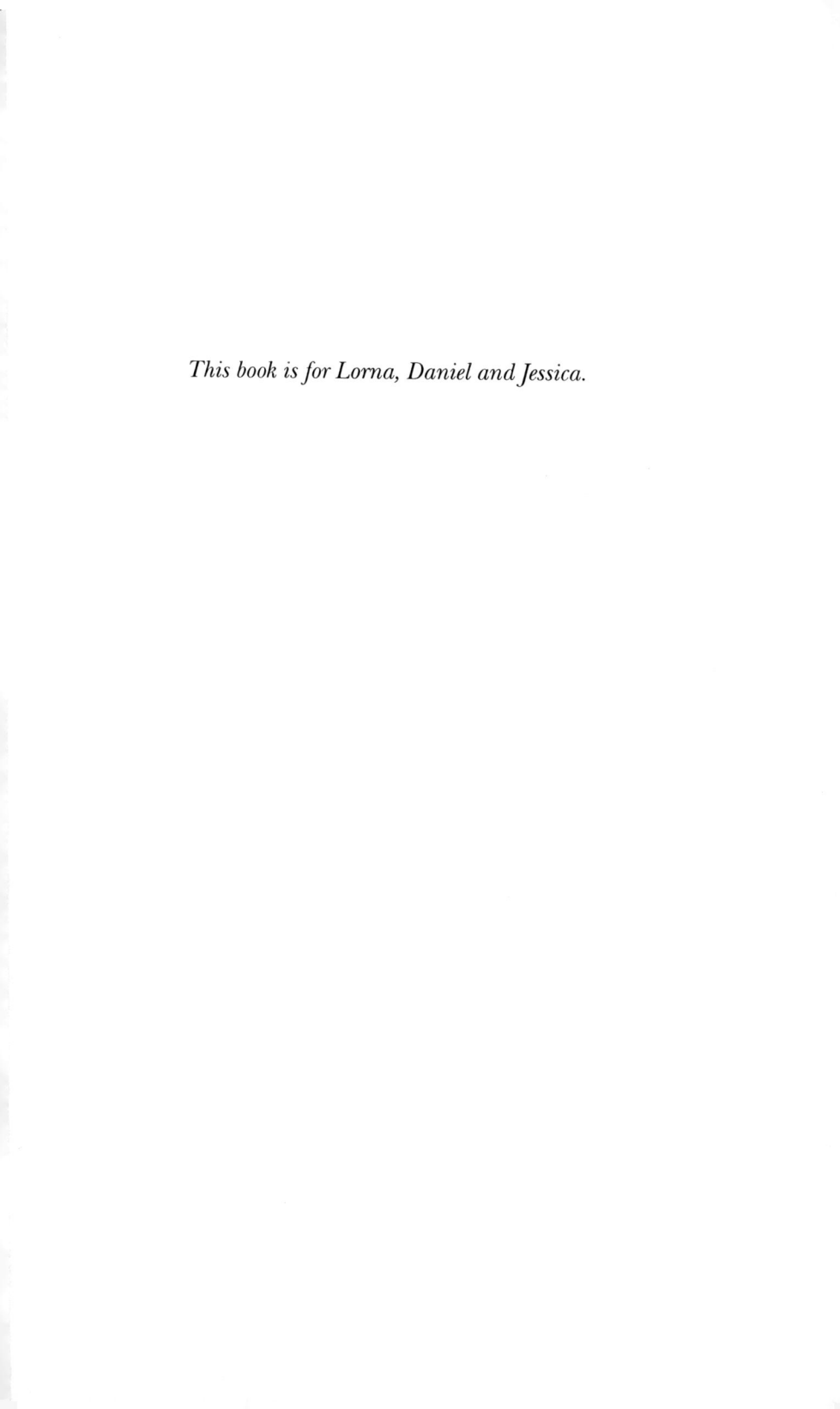

ACKNOWLEDGMENTS

Grateful acknowledgment is made to the editors of the following journals and anthologies in which these poems originally appeared:

American Poetry Review, The Centennial Review, The Humanist, The Huron Review, The Massachusetts Review, New York Quarterly, The Nation, New York Poetry, Open Places, Connections, Poets on Surviving, Manhattan Poetry Review, The Connecticut Poetry Review, The Third Eye, The Croton Review, Sub Rosa, Beloit Poetry Journal, Jewish Chronicle: Literary Supplement, The Pen, Talus, Outloud, Pembroke Magazine, 10th Decade, Prospect Review, Antigonish Review, Rialto, Ploughshares, Poetry Wales, Confrontation, Ignite, Full Bleed, Global City Review, The Laurel Review, House Organ, Rattapallax, Reflections: The United Nations, Society of Writers Magazine, PoetryBay, Ararat, Magazine.Art, Medicinal Purposes, BigCityLit, The Bear River Review, Home Planet News, Pequod, La Traductiere: Review Franco-Anglaise, Suffle Boil: A Magazine of Poetry and Music, Brilliant Corners, Portulan bleu, Lips, Ateliers de Traduction, House Organ, Same, http://jumparts.org/poetry1.html, The Manhattan Review, Creative Insight, Poets USA.com, Heliotrope: A Journal of Poetry, The Blue Jew Yorker, New Contrast, and *Jacket.* A group of 13 poems were translated into Chinese and appear in the anthology, *Selected Poems of Post-Beat Poets,* edited by Vernon Frazer [2008].

I wish to express my heartfelt thanks to the following residencies for providing the time and peace to pursue my writing: The McDowell Colony, New Hampshire, Hawthornden Castle, Scotland, Fundación Valparaiso, Spain, Casa Zia Lina on Elba, Italy, and the Monastery at Saorge, France, and to Jean-Jacques Boin, director.

CONTENTS

Author's Note / xv

from *Beast is a Wolf with Brown Fire* [1977]

Withdrawal Symptoms / 19
A Loss of Parts / 20
Skimmer / 21
A Field of Questions / 22
Another Question / 23
Deception / 24
Beast is a Wolf with Brown Fire / 25
Snake / 26
A Sleeping Man / 27
A House in the Mountains / 28
Love Poem / 29
The Legend of the Wild West / 30
The Falling Apart of Time / 31
Paranoia / 32
All Messed Up / 33

from *Roller Coaster Kid* [1982]

Roller Coaster Kid / 37
The City Rat / 41

from *Love and Crush* [1992]

Going On / 45
Love and Crush / 46
Already / 47
Not Yet the Child / 48
Four Weeks to Birth / 49
Mother / 50
Ghosts / 52
Cages / 53
Two 14-Year-Olds from City Jail / 54

Living the Life / 57
World's End Café / 58
Nightmares of the Very Young / 59
The War / 60
At Ground Zero / 61
The Fire / 62
Irangate / 63
The Power of Prayer / 64
Visiting / 65
In the Breadth of the Drum / 66
Personal Plea / 67
Lucky Man / 68
In the Hand of the Princess / 69
Monkey Talk / 70
This Quiet Moment / 71

from *The Short Life of the Five Minute Dancer* [1993]

The Short Life of the Five Minute Dancer / 75
In Case You Missed It / 76
Grim Presence / 77
Tears / 78
Life of the Mole / 79
Mother / 80
They Say / 81
Perspective / 82
Jessie at 8 / 83
Brain Damage / 84
Tony's Complaint / 85
The Careful Bump / 86
Anger / 87
A Lonely Tree / 88
Where I Need to Be / 89
Rescue / 90
And Now for the Music / 91

from *A Measure of Conduct* [1999]

A Measure of Conduct / 95

Apostrophe to Dr. Trope, Anesthesiologist / *96*
A Turn of Events / *98*
Ghosts 2 / *101*
Waking to the Dark / *102*
Androgyne / *103*
The Danger of Sarah Jones / *104*
Role Reversal / *105*
In These Times/ Charity / *106*
Devil Design / *107*
Failure / *108*
Peach Pie / *109*
Another Salesman / *110*
Father at 85 / *112*
Jessie Beforehand / *113*

from *Tony's World* [2010]

Tony Upbraids Himself / *117*
Tony Takes a Hammer… / *118*
Tony's Blade / *119*
Tony's Head / *120*
Tony's Preferences / *121*
Tony the City Booster / *122*
Little Bestiary / *123*
Tony to His Mother / *124*
Tony's Dad / *125*
Tony Cleans the Stove / *126*
Tony Practices / *127*
Tony Visits Hotel Splendide / *128*
The Day of Withholding / *130*
Tony to His Creator / *131*
That was Then; Now is Paid For / *132*
As Per Intent / *133*

Drastic Dislocations: New Poems

1. Euphoria Ripens
The Fabulous Backdrop / *139*
Under the Branches / *140*

The Bullhorn   /   *141*
Commitment to a Fog   /   *142*
Sounds Above the Monastery   /   *143*
The Nightmare   /   *144*
Shades of Keats   /   *145*
Do the Dead?   /   *146*
His Precarious Mood   /   *147*
Grains of Sand   /   *148*
   1. Euphoria Ripens
   2. Grains of Sand Again
   3. Mortality
   4. October 24th 2009: Daylight Savings Time
Items of the Grave   /   *152*
Minus a Wheelbarrow   /   *153*
"Lifey/Deathy": Sewer and Tree   /   *154*
The Old Man   /   *155*
The Excesses of Advancing Age   /   *156*
Paradise Lane   /   *157*
Prayer   /   *158*

2. Drastic Dislocations

Pandemonium   /   *161*
The Job   /   *162*
Serving the State   /   *163*
Days of the Week   /   *164*
Baggage   /   *165*
Drastic Dislocations   /   *166*
Distant Music   /   *167*
Waters Rising   /   *168*
   1. The Rain
   2. Gazing at Raindrops
The Subject   /   *170*
Cleansing Ritual   /   *171*
The Killers Again   /   *172*
Anger, a Personal History   /   *173*

3. Lorelei

What's Now   /   *177*
Lorelei   /   *178*

The Invitation / *179*
Lost / *180*
Letter to My Daughter / *181*
The Diamond Dealer's Lament / *182*
Lover / *183*
Ballad / *184*
Old Friends / *185*
A Man / *186*
Ode / *187*
Inside Our Heads: Devil Design / *188*
Sex Ghazal / *189*
Bartering / *190*
I Think / *191*
Llosa's Bad Girl / *192*
The Man Upstairs / *193*
The Circus Man / *194*
Daily Grief / *196*
Touch / 197

4. Jazz
Listening / *201*
Phone Calls to Make / *202*
Bigs and Littles / *203*
Backstage / *204*
Blue Smoke Above the Bandstand… / *205*
Blues Again / *207*
Postmodernism / *208*
Petulance / 209
Portrait / *210*
Jack the Hat / *211*
A Bunch of Could Haves / *212*
Drinking / *213*
Under the Spell of Muggles / *214*
In the Parlance of Mezz / *215*
A Man in Trousers / *217*
Blues 1 / *218*
Blues 2 / *219*
The Mafia Was on Strike; Go Ask Pacos / *220*
Rabbits on Castle Grounds / *221*

AUTHOR'S NOTE

Before I was in high school, I loved the rhymes, rhythms and images found in the collections of poetry for children: Eugene Field, especially "Wynken, Blinken and Nod," Keats' "The Naughty Boy," the lyrics of Walter de la Mare and of course, Lewis Carroll. Then, in a halting self-conscious way, I tried to write my own poems, perhaps not consciously realizing that with poetry I could express emotional truth, albeit in a disguised manner.

My commitment to study poetry, and then to practice it with some seriousness, began under the tutelage and influence of the late critic, poet and teacher, M. L. Rosenthal. He encouraged a love for what he called "the real thing" in poetry, which over the years I've tried to identify and find. Along with my gratitude for his inspiration and guidance, I want to thank the poets and friends who have been gracious and helpful readers of my poems over many years; the example of their own writing or simply their presence in my life has been a sustaining gift. These people include the late David Rosenthal, John Tytell, James Emanuel, M. L. Liebler, Daniel Leary, Stephen Watson, D. H. Melhem, Kirpal Gordon, Vernon Frazer, Bob Burr, Richard Tillinghast, Alicia Ostriker, Ruth Valentine, Marilyne Bertoncini, F. D. Reeve, and of course, Lorna Harbus Wallenstein.

I am most grateful to Raymond Hammond and NYQ Books for publishing this book as well as my previous publishers for allowing me the opportunity reprint and revise poems written and published decades ago.

BEAST IS A WOLF WITH BROWN FIRE

POEMS BY
BARRY WALLENSTEIN

FOREWORD BY M.L. ROSENTHAL

Withdrawal Symptoms

Slowly I enclose myself
by turning off the T.V.
and then standing still
& turning on the radio for safety
& then standing still
and removing to a room with less radio volume
& finally I slowly turn off the radio
& gradually, that is by stages
I pull down the shades
and bind my vision to diminished space.

    In this place
    the story begins
    with a man looking at television
    a grown man standing still
    in the center of his poem.

A Loss of Parts

All my healthy parts commune
and the stalking shape of things to be
runs through my arms
and down my wrists
and out my fingers
spoiling my healthy mouth.

> *My whole being dreams of water.*
> *A boy's face is wet, available and healthy.*
> *At school his lessons attack his health;*
> *it's the same old story.*

Four parts left.
Who goes there? What's the look?
Three parts left. How many names?
I've two good eyes—healthy parts.
But the darkening shape of things to be
brawls round my spine and spoils the space I fill.

Skimmer

I am a small skimmer, flat,
not quite a rock
and light enough to curve in the air.

The hand tosses out—
I fly off on a bent course
and lightly skim across the water
from the shallows to the deep,
skipping—hitting my shadow,
leaving it—hitting my shadow.
Tossed right, I could hit so many times.

The light skip of the skimmer
flying across the water
could be almost silent swift and gay.
When I hit my shadow in the end,
I'll plunge, make noise, and drown it.
Foolish heart! In the end, I'm neither light nor gay, but deep.

A Field of Questions

Now you tell me—
what do I look at
and what do I look like
and what do I take and how often
to feel straight now, here or
among the goldenrod?

And where do I go in my dreams?
Back to the boy sublime?
Back to the licking love?
Or back to the corner sucking a root?

Now I ask you,
when the sun is almost down
less hot and the colors deepen,
what do I need to stand upright in the elements
now—now, as the colors go?

Another Question

Are you the type, who, at 2 A.M.
when all the good stuff's gone
longs for just five more minutes
before the day is done?

Or do you curse the day
and be glad it's over,
wish the next one gone too,
clear into next week?

At bedtime, do you balance between
just enough despair to feel alive
and the desire, sharp as light,
to last long, longer than the night?

Deception

November, and the flies
are rushing into the house to die.
I'm told it's the poison in the house
that makes them die the way they do.
In September I put out poison for the mice
and sprayed the wasps and the eaves they nest in.
I wasn't thinking about flies at the time.

Now it's happened, and I wonder
would they do better in the cold?
Where could they scavenge?
Who would know them?
What of one alone?
Who could hear the solitary buzz?

November, and the late-born flies
come to the house to die.
You hardly ever see them alive.
They stop at the corners.

One just buzzed near me but
I'm young and healthy here.
I do not listen to flies.

Beast is a Wolf with Brown Fire

runs across meadows
and bounds up into
old farms, now stubbly
and overgrown.
she runs through brush
she rests among the evergreen
and the poplar.
her eyes are pinned to the light
flickering through the leaves.
she pants white mist, she lounges,
she changes sex in the shadows
and emerges in red fire.

the beast is a wolf and
she goes to you
she's found you out
my love.

Snake

She wants snake
to shake her next.

First it was some grave story,
a fairytale told at bedtime.

Then it was real life with a boy,
a hayride, gaiety, warfare!

Then she got serious,
married, solved her problems,
solved his problems,
gave birth to a life's problems.

Now she wants snake.

>   SNAKES:
>   As a girl she'd find them
>   crazy in the long grass
>   at mowing time.
>   She'd pick one up,
>   green or brown
>   always soft-bellied and frightened.
>
>   Even as a child she knew
>   they'd get mangled
>   when the mower rode by.
>
>   She didn't ever see herself
>   as a savior of snakes
>   or in any way
>   important to them
>   no matter how she loved them.
>   Now she wants snake
>   to shake her back.

A Sleeping Man

While sucking into you
I discovered a sleeping man,
a man dreaming of music.
He awoke and denied the dream—
my disturbance.

So I sought your eyes
and saw my own small face.
I shut my eyes, and disappeared.

I am folded in a kind of sleep
my angel,
and the music is as soft
as your surrounding.

A House in the Mountains

While you do nothing you can enjoy life
like sitting under the apple tree
cider there enough to cure
the cold wind passing by;
or lie back with eyes closed against
the sun and winds of autumn
and the comfort of a warm house;
wood tire logs waiting and soon
to burn and crackle against the winds
that aim at the mountains.

A house in the mountains,
you can enjoy yourself and do nothing
with hours of watching a valley
move through colors and into the dark.
And do nothing
slowly touch the dry leaves the cold stone
or the roughly velveted mosses
enjoy the silence
and the separate sounds of the wind.

The winds are moving the mountains.
Do nothing. Move as slowly as…
taste whatever taste that makes you move,
no matter how slowly, to the ever dying peace.
Enjoy the peace.
The winds may do nothing.
The house is tight. Some peace will last.

      And do nothing enjoy life
      all clover
      sitting pretty
      in the catbird's seat
      you needn't move
      en   joy u   self.

Love Poem

You wouldn't dare touch us now
    as we pass by in sunshine
    after a summer rain
    as we hold each other 'round.
Such is the dazzling –

You wouldn't move toward us
    for at this moment
    our private life
    has all the world in sway.

But
these conceits
are sprung from terror,
for in the woods
behind my house
a hooded man casts about –
he's known and lying low.

I've bolted the doors.
I've my position;
he has his reasons.

The Legend of the Wild West

Around these parts
her caress is as famous as death.
It's told she holds her men for the kill
and never gets measured herself.
But, having come a long way,
with nothing else to do in the town,
I stepped a pace and looked her up
and she led me in   all softness
and covered my mouth
as if to silence caution.

Then, and slowly, she worked her fingers into my mouth.
              I thought it was sex.
              It might have been murder.
And if I hadn't been clued
by one who knows
I'd still be calling her death-lock, love.
So just as the town ends
I too left clean glad to be alive and breathing.

You see, on some dull evening, when there is no TV,
it's occurred to me that every touch is the touch of death,
the marking out of the mortal flesh,
wanting, through touching, to break skin,
to annihilate the flesh by celebrating it.
So, I imagined the wild west;
in such a place the town ends suddenly
and clearly, and everything beyond is wild and clean.

The Falling Apart of Time

My brain is beside me
or on the glass table
looking or itself looking like
a dropped watch.

Everywhere, I mean near me,
the parts
or loose connections fall about.
A wheel is moving or rolling
into an object which collapses.

That too takes time.

My grandfather's watch
was gold.
It ran through him through all the states
into a long pocket,
his gentleman's trousers.

In more recent times,
I do the watch trick:
my smallest hand, the second hand,
falls off;
my crystal, all in fragments,
catches light & cuts.
And my movements,
all my fine movements,
my jewels and bearings,
wind down and spring shut.

Paranoia

Think of something soft: wool
lambs wool
angel hair—
you know if you inhale
these things will kill.

So reconsider the soft
choking you get wise.
Think of the pragmatic
steel
cast-iron
or lead.
But
if turned against you
these things too will kill.

So you're confused
and ever watchful, lest
some sharp blow undo you.
You hardly ever sleep.
You hire a taster for your food
and outside
you never spit
into the wind.

All Messed Up

You're all messed up
When in spite of the neatness of your hair
 you find that in order to do
a day's good work
you need a month to rest
a week to move
and another week to finish up

also
if you can't get out the door and
if when you do
you come back with infections

you might be bad but
if you check the mirror and
you're still neat
if you're not too impolite
then you may walk straight.

I mean, my brother,
you can straighten up
walk out
and carry on.

Roller Coaster Kid

He's been up there for five days,
this oddball, this roller coaster wiz;
he's ridden 700 miles of track.

About a week ago
he appeared like a ghost
and asked if he could ride for free
after paying for the first four rides.
Now, how do you answer that?
So we agreed.

There's so many freaks around.
These thin boys with dull stares
or stars in their eyes,
I can't follow it.
They come to the shows,
they hang around.
This one too,
he wasn't any different.
I figured he'd try to be a big shot
and show off with six or seven rides
to show his friends he's man and can stand the speed.

Well, he fooled us,
and now all the reporters are getting on us,
and all the people are hating us.
They hate us because they imagine things;
they love to make us the weirdest stories.
Yet they pay
and they watch the kid
ride the roller coaster
over and over and over and over.

He might be a wonder of some sort
some sort of mystical person
like you read about in books.
I mean, 700 miles of track is a lot of distance.
The speeds are enough to make you dizzy watching.
If you want to know the truth
I can't help liking the kid.
All things aside, he set his mind
on doing something and he's doing it.

It's a funny business
lots of oddballs
lots of hustlers.

And now this kid.
He knows he's drawing the crowds.
He knows he's a smash on the roller coaster
and he probably thinks he can make a deal.

Well, I'm no fool.
I've seen dollars
when they were dimes.
I don't make bad deals.
He got his free rides;
children bring him food at
the few slow spots.
Imagine the nerve
this kid off the street
stars in his eyes
and he wants every penny I've got.

On the other hand he is bringing 'em in
and he's a good-looking kid
sturdy and with lots of potential.
He might make good.

Imagine, if things work out
we could go on the road.
We'd make all the big cities
stay in the best hotels
share everything fifty-fifty.
There's no telling...

> *(His face flashes by*
> *a streaming white flash*
> *dark cars shine against the sky.)*

I can't tell anymore
for he's made no offer.
He seems to like the ride
just for the ride.
Maybe he's holding out!

Watch him.
Every time he whips by
his face changes.
I mean every time he passes by me
that smile he wears for his friends
changes to a stare at me
a stare that could drive a man crazy.

You've got to watch these kids—
either they're weirdoes or hustlers
or thieves or fairies or reds
or greens or yellows or
purple or orange or pears
or twins or monsters or
movies or television or
soda pop
soda pop
soda pop
pop pop

The City Rat

The rat frightens even
the rails underground
at 59th and Lex.

No one wants to see it,
yet its speed
its hurry out of sight
chills the spine.

Close up, dead or alive,
the smell will stop your breath.

Poor rat, so ugly,
so full of evil promises,
if fools sing your praises,
I'm one
and want to know where have you been
and where are you going.

LOVE AND CRUSH

POEMS BY

Barry Wallenstein

Going On

Summertime is at the eventide,
and I am released and struck now
by the slow effort which shows
as you rise and walk from there to here.
Late in the day for you
and therefore for us all.

Tomorrow afternoon all the children
with imagination
will bolt upright
and sensing the full sway
of the great years
of lust and scrounging—
will shiver at the power in the old folks
and feel their own bones turn
the spinning hoop
as they wish
       rush through
       the gathering grace of—
       going on.

Love and Crush

All the life we love
leaves soon to feed
some other life
other love.

Thus the vigilance of the dinner hour:

The inchworm, thriving on leaves,
defoliates at times and is off;
the beetle, the aphid—that crowd—
threaten every berry bush, every fruit tree;
the woodworm, devious,
feels like, looks like
its own meal (crushed pulp)
and the ants all over
swarming by the tree root
will spread out
and draw the eye from the tree.

The centuries brood around the table.
No need to crush or rush
this balanced diet
as we, provender, make our way.

Already

Beneath mother's tent
there swims a developing youth movement
lately from the land of dreams
soon to become a riot
and already
my mysterious fish
you have joined me
in the inbetween land.

We are both hurtling back
    you from
    me to
that place you've already forgotten
that place I've heard talk of.

Little ripple
out of this solemn mood
I call to you.

Not Yet the Child

Baby
in the amniotic dream
circles and bumps:
no papers, prints on record
nothing yet
in the eyes of the law.
My eyes are wild.

This fish without a name
carries the light
we cannot yet read by.

Four Weeks to Birth

Our genes are hiding
in the belly of a fish
in the skin of a belly
in the belly of a fish
floating glyphs
micro-hints of dancing ghosts.

So much to come to life
all at once!
A resurrection of
a history of laugh-lines, hair-lines,
birthdays.

Grandpa's to come back
carrying what item
what promise of his esteem?
And the others nudge forward
through the hordes, toward our love.

Hilarious mayhem in the blood
with you now on your way.

Mother

My mother was born
inside an angel cake
did well
to dwell
in the darkness,
but, pressured,
she ate herself out
into the light.
Thus, I was born.

So, for some years
we both, pleased, ignored shadows
and never each other.
I don't remember just how long.
But one day
on a subway platform
I ran from her hand up the steps
and through the streets.
I was fleet and confused
so I wasn't caught
until out of breath & crying
she reached me properly,
took me home, gently.

I became a flame unto myself
and that too spread.
I tried to set the house afire.

The help I received
was the help I called for;
I'd call out still
but for the shields
and the shields of fortune.
Some day mother will sit

within an angel choir,
some days in fine voice,
on others, a shrinking violet.
Given a cloudless day,
she may look down on me
looking up her way,
my eyes clear and moistened
by her warm feathers,
the bright sight of her wings.

Ghosts

Yes, I'm one of them,
a shade up from some past life,
one of many, visiting.
Tonight you ask
am I an early or late emanation?

You hold me closely
as I pass among
those prior kickers
drunk and untied
fading from current ills
lingering in distant miasma and
rising again
through the centuries, ribboning.

And you persist:
might I be a final version
as you loosen your hold?
Each time when I emerge through the elements,
each time enthralled,
I'm brought to earth by questions
prickling my ears
teasing my touch
making me doubt my new formed self.

Cages

In some people's cages
you can see a smile so rare
you'd want to be there
right inside forever
share that smile
and behind the owner's back
live the life of the cage.

Once at a friend's house
I saw a smile was on fire;
it melted the bars and took us in.
In each other's eyes—stillness.
We saw flesh softening
but we didn't stay long
we had to rush out of
away from
that terrible lure.

Two 14-Year-Olds Talking from City Jail

In the cold grey ward
bothered by no one finally
the boy and girl sit
on two separate cots
—she visiting; he entertaining:

> when I get outa here
> I'm going to Canada
> once there I'll do one last job
> —enough to buy a house
> and a car
> and some easy time

and she said
> hey, check you out

and he talked past that

> I'll even go fishing
> —any day man, I mean
> what the shit
> I've been takin' it
> all this time

(he shows the half-starved waif
his bruises, where they nearly
flayed the skin off his back)

> yeah! I'm gonna get up there

and she, half a tear caught
in the corner of her lips
said
> hey, check you out

and he drew on his cigarette hard
and didn't say anything
for a long while
and then he said

> maybe after I get out
> after I serve this time
> before I head north
> I'll see Sharon one more time
> yeah, I'll see Sharon again
> check that out sweet stuff
> what d'ya think?

well (she said) well...
and laughed softly with no meanness
and she nodded her head
with a sad tick
and didn't say anything else.

And for the first time
since she was let in
he stood up
and with a bow, a smile and a wink
he took his cigarette all the way in
to his mouth
and rounding his broken lips
blew smoke rings out
and with his tongue
he flicked the butt
onto the cement floor
and with just the toe of his shoe
he ground it out.
She sat there
pulling a loose thread
from her sleeve.

Finally she got up
and stood for a last hug

>Listen
>don't worry about me
>who loses things anyway
>it's a joke anyway

if you're inside, you're inside
and if you're on the outside
that's just another chance.

Living the Life

I just peed
and there wasn't any blood

that doesn't make any difference—
I'm just as good as
Claudia, Susan or the man
they call Nick the Final Blaster

what floats by on the calm surface
need not be shot at
but if it happens
and the duck (in pieces) dies
who's going to make the front pages
"...shot for resisting..."
something

these are the times violence
kisses itself all over
there is not enough gas in the ground
to suck up

I go in a house
where the quietest rooms hum with
the planning of some
hypothetical forward action
and I go out in the air
and it's the same thing
some days

World's End Cafe

Where do the hunted, the sadly haunted
run to right before
they're called out
made to stand on some line
and tell truths about
why they ran
and what they were doing
either sitting around (dodgy-eyed)
or pacing back and forth
in a closed room (buttons and switches)
with no windows overlooking the sea.

No view at all
for those bent over
no freshening sea breezes
on those necks, those dirty dirty necks
and no matter how alive the mind
how ready the wit
—agile fingers
scratching ass
—the eyes made up
to look younger,
they remain on line and taking questions.

Still, they don't give in.
They ooze what they ooze
slaving for the trials
slithering from the trials
into silence and the dark cells.
Theirs is the dream of running always
out of the tight room, out of the hour
to some time long ago
or ahead to where the line doesn't end.

No holiday light left
in those still beautiful human eyes.

Nightmares of the Very Young

Every minute, each tick of the night
all over the world,
tens of thousands of four-year-olds
are shocked loose from dreaming:
hot and squinched, they lie
not cute,
their small teeth grinding.

Some free spirits pitch their screams
high and loud enough
to crack even the glassy eyes
of the night spectres.

Others, though, stifle their cries;
savvy, they dare not call out
for fear they'll disturb and quicken
what plunges through the darkness
towards their beds.

Thus they grip themselves around
and soon squeeze back into the dream
where, wriggling there, they're safer
thrashed and tied
than bashed and shamed above.

The War

I knew
this would be the last thing done on earth.
I sensed, I knew too that too soon
I'd die.

Weeks before the war began
I started scrubbing myself—showering
two, three times a day—washing my hands
over and over.
I was clean before
                            hop
but then I knew
into the cleanest creases
of my worried skin
something was up and soon to be over.

                         hop hop
Now I'm a frog
grounded beneath twisted
already rusted, pitted steel.
Each time the blasts thunder
(and the broiling heat)
I dive into whatever mud's left,
flick my tongue at whatever flies,
some mite fallen off its wing
and swallow.
No joy in the poisoned meal.

My spots have been gone for hours.
I'm sticky skin drying
and all of a sudden blind.

At Ground Zero

Far outside the warren
where rabbits cuddle around their paws
and a myriad of insects tick and intuit
the chemical change,
a rumbling crash comes down.
A tower falls, from old age,
earthquake or detonation?
Some terrible spreading timbre
no one knows.

Inside, where they breathe
close to the animals
hear the tiniest sweetest coos and sighs
and the hard rubbings of fur.
But step back from the creatures
and your antique mouth
is dropped by the booms
constant and nearing
old age falling down
hearts stopped
by the giant flares
coming at last to, the heart
to the snug places
where even toward the final hour
fresh droppings flavor the soil.

The Fire

> *The fix-it man can't fix everything,*
> *no one can—only fire.* —Daniel, 3 ½ years old

Snow white moth before me
seems all wings, lacelike
with filament thin feelers.
Tonight they fail in the real world,
fragile and in need of heat,
they fly into the candle flame.

So too my own life spills toward fire:
My life, my city, state
the whole region of life
crackling, slimy, scorched deeply
finally.

What does a rooster know
pecking near a common fence,
the paint flecking from the wood?
My foot against the ground
makes a startling sound
which makes the bird go round
in a fluff of wings.
The colors sunburst red and brown;
even the straw on which the rooster struts
is dyed and deeply beautiful.

The moth in flight,
the animal in the yard:
as you read
there is no great or grave fire.

Irangate (or Big Guns)

The big man sells guns
to a little man
who pays cash to another little man
who's hung up on the big man, being
a little middle man
a pocket man
a pocket
who buys more guns from the big man
to sell to another little man
who needs to shoot &
otherwise prove himself strong to

folks who eat beans
& would rather water a seed
than be tied backward on a rack, a wheel
that turns the engines in the heart
of that big man & all those
directly plugged into his arse
getting fatter—less little
with every meal, deal

fart.

The Power of Prayer

It was the day the dust refused to desist
swirling blinding the one-eyed
and the two-eyed alike.
No one in the town had prayed
for anything like this.
Someone outside the town surely must have.

Visiting

My head unscrews itself
and floats off into the next room
where, careless of gravity, it gracefully
ascends to the ceiling.

There it hangs out in a high corner
ears tucked against the right angle
eyes look down on a man
asleep on a large bed
miserable
pinched eyes and occasional twitches.
Only the jaw is relaxed—mouth agape:
some drugged spittle dries white
on the upper lip.

I want to return to my body
in the other room.
What made leave that form I know?
It too can lie down, die, dim again
and light up springing.
Everything, in fact, that goes on here
can take place there as well.

In the Breath of the Drum

It wasn't her smooth slick bright
sports car
or the yellow tinge 'twixt her teeth
that won my sighs, my spells,
my body one time I say,
nor was it
her healing strokes;
nothing so gentle crossed my mind.
It was her gaze (the long kind)
at my sister looking down
that set me up bright
for what she'd do
between this room and tomorrow.

Personal Plea

You don't look like your daddy
you don't look like your daddy

You don't smell like fish
you don't smell like fish

Do you scare?
Were you scared?
Are you scared?

Come out of the closet
dark and crowded
his long coats
her furs
everything shrouded.

(Why did they keep the phone in there?
The ring was so faint
unless you heard it, hiding.)

It's over young man
and you're just tired.

The phone number's changed
and they're gone
and the furs are gone.

It's stuffy, unhealthy in there;
turn around and come out

you original!

Lucky Man

OK—so you're free at your work,
a gentle terror getting ahead—very lucky.
Everyone sharpens up to your face,
no one bothers your time.

The ride home beats the traffic,
you're in a controlled skid.
When the sun gleams off the river,
sunshades glide you safely home.

Home
pure grain gin—lemon
the afternoon's free—every turn's a free turn
the phone's on machine.

>   Lucky
>   you never skin a shin
>   hurt a hair
>   or bother moving things aside
>   but take care
>   if you don't cheat that luck
>   it will kiss you back
>   and you'll spend all of your
>   last ten years
>   as some other person's
>   sad memory.

In the Hand of a Princess

I'll write for you
you hold me in three fingers
as you would an ordinary pen
but I'm not you know
for you I'm special
my glide would be
—if I had them—
lightning sparks
in your mind
so you love me—smile
at my dulling point
naughty of you
to slide me behind your ear
beneath golden perfumed ringlets
can't write a straight line
(who says that—
your mind or mine?)
then in a pensive frame
you chew my nub—oooh
the length of my life depends
on the thoughtful pressure of your hand
and the teasing bite of your teeth.

Monkey Talk

"Lately," the monkey says
"when I get into bed with
reclining monkeys,
the two I love,
(on different spots on the clock
and in different corners)
each one sleeps
most of the time I'm there.

So I fuss about the cage and swing,
simulating happiness
rung to rung,
and I roll into the tire
hanging from a long cord
and swing around and around
way past dizzy.
When the circling stops,
I try to focus
on the dozing monkeys,
and I fall asleep.

Sometimes, I dream my fingers
are digging beneath their fur, soft,
and hard are the lice I pick out
to quickly chew."

This Quiet Moment

The few I know—so clearly now,
so close, are asleep
and I, cracked in two and miles away
from half myself,
from half this resting, slowly pulsing
population

sit awake
(like the police)
more alone than before,
and I admit their sleepy breathing
ever this gently
in their dreaming:
little sighs—timed zzz zzzz apart.
I walk over and visit one,
just one;
then, in my mind another and another and another,
(that's enough!)
and I bend over to straighten a sheet,
cover a shoulder,
kiss her forehead,
slip beside—.
No invasion; this brief visit in the dark
is over.

Hardly a sound is coming off the street
in New York City—
Part of this quiet is a hummm,
city-deep, continuous,
sinuous. And now a distant siren—
Police who never sleep
wait like me
for something tight to wake up
and be restless;
someone delightful at the end of the night
to contend with,
this one.

THE SHORT LIFE OF THE 5 MINUTE DANCER

POEMS BY

Barry Wallenstein

The Short Life of the Five Minute Dancer

I'm six hours absent all day long
like a weasel in winter in a tree,
deaf to the world:
I drift in the haze, latent, secretive,
absently waiting to dance and do
for five minutes at a time.
You, my doctor,
watch me last
for five minutes at a time.

Then watch me fade into
the six-hour haze.
Sniff the way I breathe.
Deep in the haze I'm fine,
so fine in fact I'm fed through veins.

Now watch again closely:
I'm the dark speck drifting in the luminous sky,
the sudden recognition that all is not well,
the restive hour that spends the day,
the thing that will not scare
until—
I burst out to dance
for five minutes.
I last the while in the grandest style,
you—you watch me do
for five minutes at a time.

In Case You Missed It

here it comes again:

The man walked across the bridge
very slowly
—like a star moving
against a ribbon
in the sky—
very long, the bridge, it was
very high
and the wind rolling along his back,
flapping at his coat tails,
snapping against his trousers.

The iron railings are cold
and he avoids holding on
lest his hands freeze and stick.
He leans over the rail
he leans and stares
at the black invitation
flowing and churning—as if
there were a motor beneath
and an army of operators
all with families
working under the water
for pleasure;
he hears a promise

before—in the air

in case you missed it.

Grim Presence

My one grim friend
with the grudge of a nation
12 times defeated,
how did I earn your attention?
Somehow, sadly,
I got caught in your eye.

Here I am
helpless on your pupil,
and I don't like it!
If I could also be
the cotton swab to gently remove
the agonizing speck I've become,
how glorious and easy that would be.

Tears

for David Rosenthal

There are tears in the water
the water can't fathom;
the fish, the reptiles,
the larger clans, are all disturbed;
distanced from themselves,
they fall dumb.

Off to the side
I build a casket.
Others of my kind wait, tensing,
and when the wind strikes the vane
they weep in profusion.

What melts in the sea
and settles so deeply?

What soft cloth,
wrapped round the head of the boy,
will cushion his gentle recline?

The Life of a Mole

for David Rosenthal

There are moles burrowing,
making their way,
silently riding, scurrying, gliding
on glistening claws.
Faced by a box, they hesitate.
But soon, the texture is familiar,
with an odd taste fleeting, after.
And then there are the brass handles.

Apart from, yet near to
these craven, careless, chewing creatures
and their startled eyes,
there are other eyes, quiet,
staring through, canceling out
the channeling moles.

Mother

1.

the mourning after mother died
my mouth tasted metal
my breath turned foul
a week later I blew a kiss
at her grave and the grave-flowers died

the moon browned above me
and I felt her fall more deeply downwards

2.

Before this happened Mother was first
in one place and then in another
always limited, however concentrated

Now she's everywhere, a film of power
Father's abandoned
while she spills her favors like stardust
equally on all of us who think

3.

My children just wandered out of sight
far down the park's lane
Mother, watch them for me
Grandmother you are, don't doze
don't be too still
I trust them to come back
slightly more than I don't trust
the park
to let them return

They Say

the homeless are tearing apart the bridges
in New York City.
Their need for firewood outstrips
the bridges' capacity to give.

Consider phantom bridges,
darkened dangerous roadways,
feeder roads going nowhere,
and the fires being kept
and everyone
warm along the waterfront,
under the rusting trestles
of this fine city.

Gone are the great and graceful spans of light.

Action:
the iron helmets need to know:
which ones of you
pulled the wood down,
who handed what to whom,
who was there, to strike the match;
how many shielded the small flame
and fanned it larger?
How many spent the night?
The failed bridges are losing memory.

Beneath the few still grand remaining spires,
there is less,
more and more—this new milling life,
a flickering band
girding the city.

Perspective

Were I not part of us
how carefully I would point us
out: you on the telephone
and him on a lounge a hundred miles away.
I'd be jealous of both—you breaking the rules
and his complicity.
But I'm here, in front of you
involved, as it were,
in the evening;
my arms around your knees
my head for you to hold or consider.

It took a great mounting of natural events,
earth slides, mushroom growth,
before I'd slide my cheek up this way
or lose a burden this way.

If I were not part of us
I'd imagine sanctions and flight.

Jessie at 8

She concentrates on her dentistry.
She may give up the trade and its tools tomorrow,
but for now, she's engaged,
operating on two old jaws.
One is a deer's
and that's the youngest,
the freshest dead.
"The spaces between the teeth
are perfect," she says.
She pokes and picks around. She says,
"cleaning out the plaque;
gee your plaque is big"—
a certain way of talking to animals
dead or alive—friendly.

The second set of teeth is darker,
petrified, hoary from age.
No visible spaces between those dentures;
not enough jaw to identify.
She doesn't flinch
but speeds ahead to improve
what's left of a mouth.

She looks up:
"I'm the dentist of dead animals."

Brain Damage

I can go to the spigot and turn it on.
I can drink from it.
With the hose I can moisten the garden,
but I haven't the eight or nine words
that go with spigot,
words plumbers and poets must know.

So here too I'm the skimmer
hitting lightly and then
that sinking feeling.
My mind is damaged on the end of the world,
and I'm left only words
like drink and sprinkle and sparkle and spigot.

On a moonless night in the garden
I can no longer name the bright stars
or the iridescent things that fly,
but I can still feel
the hard shell of a snail
and the softer, ordinary slug.

Tony's Complaint

The world's been destroying me
with its notions
about my potions
and the ways to my pain.

Shall I shoot myself
backwards
or ahead,
down and under?

Surely
you know
notion is illegal
at the center of pain.
In my pocket there's heaven,
so please,
Mr. Cheese,
leave off!

Careful Bump

I was standing around
figuring my situation
keeping to myself, outside of trouble,
when this guy bumps me

Whammo!

Hey! I say,
watch it,
be more careful!
Careful? he says, why I'm so careful
I don't even see you.

Then I understood my situation:
The casual error of a bump,
chance collisions
set me up
and
let me down.

Anger

When anger falls on the plate like food
limp—something you wouldn't
want to eat—don't force yourself
I tell myself
let it go
the feeling of being pissed off
having been ripped off on the run
taken for a fool
some no count lame-ass crier
couldn't put a shoe in a basket on a bet
or control his own best leads
a shame to his hours
sucking on anger.

Listen, I tell myself
spit that juice
into waters widening
where the elements in waves
will wash harmless
that wrath,
the truest feeling.

A Lonely Tree

There are 12 men in the toaster
don't ya know
there are 12 men near broiling.

You should do something, but no,
the size of the men
or the size of the toaster
worries you—you talk about it
and draw into yourself
don't ya know.

Elsewhere, but not far,
there are meetings in The Emergency.
Questions spin around broiling:
should a group of heros
unplug the gadget
which took years of money to build?
If the 12 were set free,
who would they join,
where would they settle?

Would they run to the tree
to save the cat
caught in the branches
terrified and dangerous to pull down?

You pull yourself together
and laugh.
12 men in a toaster
don't ya know
and cats in a tree—true.

The temperature's broiling
and the mice, they've disappeared
don't ya know.

Where I Need to Be

Crystal coke and fine mist wine
Is where I need to be.
The devil took the lesser soul
And left the skin for me.

In fallow fields of discontent
The braggart devil lies.
His fists are tight, his movements light,
And watch how well he dies.

He comes again to take a spine,
To take a leaf and leave a stain.
His death is but a parody
of dying grief beneath the pain.

So it's cold
Beneath the wind,
And it's where I want to be,
And crystal coke
And fine mist wine
Are all that's left for me—
For the devil took the fattened soul
And left just the skin for me.

Rescue

Your hand
>across the water
>on its course—

its reach
>how it comes over
>to my side—

Does it signify
what I need
>transport?

Or is what I see
the dull familiarity of rescue?

Tremulous
>my sigh bumps the rail
>till steady.

Steady
>your grasp there
>is taken.

And Now for the Music

There's a terrible rhythm bearing down
a boy with a drum and a permanent frown
a mask on the wall which won't go away
no matter where you move
no matter how you pray.

Imagine—wearing the mask that haunts you.

So the devil floats up off the map of crime
the expensive coat and a $5 shine;
he walks and he talks to the beat of the drum
in the hands of the boy bashing,
sweating, and not yet done.

*He's average in the music, he's new
and doesn't know, this time, what to do.*

But the devil does and does his dance
arhythmic jolts in the cuts of chance;
he forgets the boy who beat the drum
in the last few hours
of the blasted sun.

Thus the world comes down
at the end of the day
in the woods—the fields
where animals play;
where men like tigers
act like spiders
weaving about, breathing upon
their ghost-like prey.

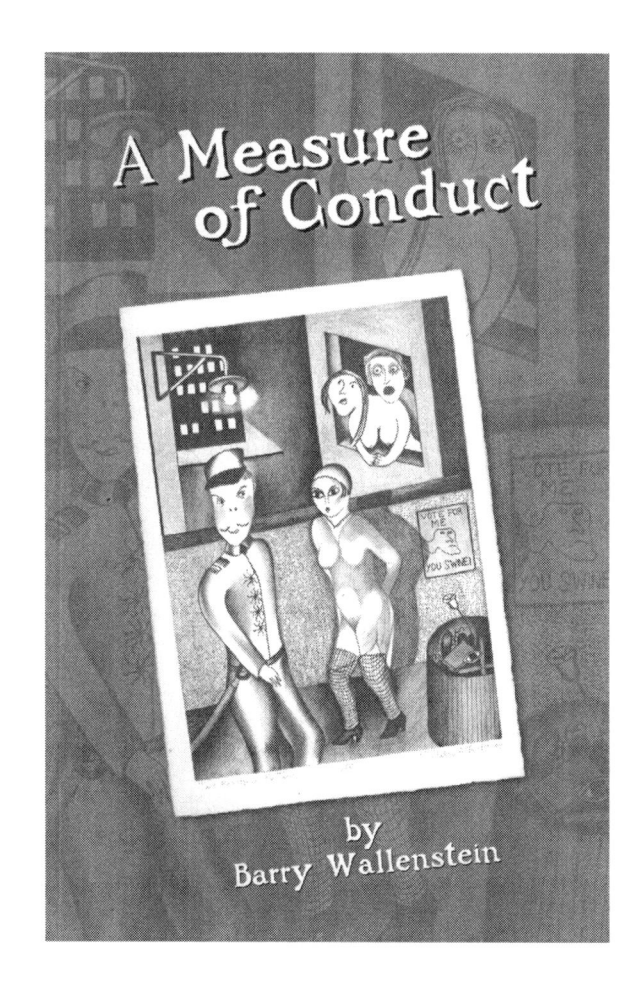

A Measure of Conduct

by
Barry Wallenstein

A Measure of Conduct

I see an earwig
on the way from the woodshed—
logs in the carrier with the creature
caught, looking like bark,
scurrying for the damp
and into the dark.
The pincers rise and dip
as I step indoors.

I stand there, near the stove,
the logs a crackling consummation,
ideas spin wildly—possessed, deathdark.
Other thoughts press for time—
consider the creature a sign,
a measure of conduct:
six legs, leathery forewing,
all instinct and woody purpose.

After such reverie
will I rescue the bug
by searching the carrier? Will I
carefully remove the logs—set each down gently,
feel around for the scuttler; locate the mini-beast,
carry him on a leaf far from the fire?
Or will I let him burn on a ride into the stove

or perhaps I'll forget what I saw—
the small thing retreating;
perhaps imagine it's saved itself,
dropped out of the canvas when I wasn't looking;
perhaps, in an absent state, I confused
action with inaction, smallness with
next to nothing.

Apostrophe to Dr. Trope, Anesthesiologist

Dear Doctor, drawn from an episode of pain,
I remember your swift manner—before the shot,
two times delivered, put me out.
I asked to be well under,
go for the luscious midnight swim,
and you smiled—I shouldn't fret;
I trusted, thrust a smile back
and went down deeply.

Meanwhile, back on the table
the other doctor cut
along the lines of his attention:
he'd gained his strength
from the Law, money, and wanting to see life
extended according to his training.
He cut so well,
made clean an area that was foul;
the promise of death, back on the shelf in hiding.

A year's gone by;
a new light flickers
and I call you back.
Where does the memory of pain hide,
the pinch that preceded your gift?
Now—I can't even find the spot
that attracted one doctor's tools
and, Dr. Trope, your skill.
From the gathering mists I raise my voice.

Dr. Trope, I've dreamed of you
standing here at my bedside—in white,
a gauze mask dangling from white thread.
I ask you about the laws of poetry, probabilities,
the range of tropes.
Do you know how many there are of you?
I'm a devil to ask:
are there little Tropes at home?
Mamma and Poppa Trope still alive?

As far as the personal,
here's a proposal:
let's take a trip, right before the onset,
your hand over my mouth,
holiday shots of liquid morphine,
my pulse watched,
my pressure—
you're the professional,
invisible—be my bride.

A Turn of Events

Smacked in the head,
the one story I remember is about killing
and lust and hatred and wonderful circumstance:
Not too long ago
at latitude y longitude x
there was a feud in progress
between the McClatchys and the Drummonds
harsh words about fences, pitchforks and finally
shot guns aimed at close range
up in the hills, barely out of town.
Then there was a lull
after some burying
and a good deal of hard staring.
The stand-off lasted days.

In another part of the world
a trio of oddly connected figures
was fidgeting about in a city room.
They'd been up high and wired for days,
believing in their own costumes:
the tomahawk haircut
on the pale slim boy
with eyes like wash
unshadowed by the blond brows,
nor do his blond lashes
soften anything;
his sleek girlfriend or sister
stands in a faux leopard top,
short black skirt way above spiked heels.
Her lips look brown or black
depending on how the light falls and shades.
That same light shimmers
the tattoo of a house on fire
on the upper left arm

of the man in the cut-off tee shirt,
three rings in his left ear.
He could be the boy's father
or older brother. The girl could be
his daughter, his bait,
his long dead wife's distant niece.

This threesome,
suffering the nudge of a dull time,
plot some random assault
on the outside world.

Destiny would find them in a small town
200 miles from the city
longitude x latitude y
set in the piney hills.
They would silently, brazenly, walk
to the peaceful home
of June and Jack Adams
and their children, Jane, 12
and the boy, Timothy, 15 and very shy.

They would surprise, with no effort,
the quartet of Adams.
They would tie up poppa
leave alone or tease momma
strike and confuse Timmy
and after eating and drinking
all the good stuff
concentrate so on Jane,
her family would pass out entirely.
It's been done—
sodomizing even the furry little pet animals
and out of anger and the feeling of being late

for some forgotten connection, suddenly recalled,
finish off the lot. As in
no more Adams family.

But instead—on their way, that day,
through the woods, towards the simple cottage
just above the town,
having ambled and bitched and planned their games,
(the boy had even sharpened his teeth,)
they stumbled on the feud,
just as the lull between the two forces
caved in:
The McClatchys and the Drummonds
fired ensemble and the cross-fire
kept the nameless citizens
formless in fact—kept them from the date
the Adams knew nothing about.

Ghosts 2

Riding hungry in a limousine,
a leather case upon my lap,
flashed a sign that hung between
salesmanship and the trap:
"Steak Stampede" it blazed,
and I, transported, imagined
"Corpses on the Run":

a ghastly drumbeat

at last the images, trailing tatters,
ribbons of slow moving forms;
the ancient dead
massed with the young—
muscle-ripplings turned blue.
Same speed; same dull ignorance of how long.

Cut—the image quickens:

running from dirt,
from cruel gravity,
the oldest the fastest,
the youngest fast too and amazed.
They dash from criminal corners
toward angels, imperfect memories;
they're dashing to flowers

    to the leather
    on the lap
    to the lap itself

    all laps finally
    entertained, shade by shade,
    by ghosts

    intemperate.

Waking to the Dark

When I awoke the day was gone
having dived, as if targeting
back into the night.
Night had been a meadow of dim figures
smoking, telling stories,
revealing under the darkened dome.

I rubbed my eyes and the screen tore
and the flies shot in
ravenous and darting for sweets.
I was that way once,
sweet pea,
or sweet anyway.

So there I lay, eyesockets and cellophane,
wondering where the morning hid.

Then, like a shy monster,
it peeked out from a corner,
dust and a pillow covering the glow;
day-glow and I kicked the pillowed dust aside
and there it was, a vision,
the room illumined—bureaus
standing like tombstones, blank
and waiting for information,
spectral arms locked outright,
tightened fists crazily aimed
at a relaxed sky.

No wonder the morning
aims back at the dark,
and the daylight finds a shroud.

Androgyne

Lonely lemon   sucked on
too little and so late at night
he/she sleeps or
lolls about on lakefront sand
affecting a languor

The soft waves
lap near her/his legs

Fast they were and
supple—
still they can stretch and bend
in a direction
sucked on all the way up and down

She/he demanded it too little
from all the respecting cousins
and reluctant friends—
should have opened up
and called for sweets

The delicate one on the chair
his/her legs crossed   smiling now
is beckoning

The Danger of Sara Jones

Collect the knives of Sara Jones
before she picks a favorite.
Remove them from her hands
as you would staunch the murderous wish
turned inward.

It's the doctor's orders.
Though you are the new boy,
you're the one to greet her,
be sweet to her and
calmly lift away the danger.

Watch, for all the treatments,
Sara still shakes her hair back
as at her own beauty—then forward;
the strands, like whip-snakes
lash across her eyes.

She doesn't bother looking our way.
Besides, being radiant and mad,
she knows, from this distance, we're watching;
stop trembling. Go!
She's by the kitchen doorway, whittling.

Role Reversal

There's this oversized pin
wriggling on the wall,
held down by a giant insect
worrying its perfectly thin steel frame.

It wishes it could bend
and prick, maybe even poison
the fearsome long-legged creature
that's been here—dominant
these long nights into the days.

Everywhere, the bugs have been aggressive,
mixing in—accurately.

Soon they will have us all impaled
unless, as in the old days (sigh),
the insects are pinned in a book
like butterflies.

Depends on the creature just where
the pin should slide through
and the background, the background
should be cold and barely visible.

In These Times/ Charity

It's a shame
the little assistance we gain
when bent over
with cramps/ills ill fortune
broke   the busted
lie down in dusted.

It's as if sustenance
had to be sucked through a straw
and always a joker in the wings
with pins ready to poke holes
a minor cruelty—
the thin forbear.

So these are the hard times
as in the old days:
the hand jerks out
hardly able not to
& whether something drops in
or not,
the local eyes are dim
and next week as blind
as the very idea.

Fish swim in the sea in schools.
Do they swim for greed out of cunning?
They do ignore what shouldn't be seen,
abandoning the faulty fish—
those with the white spots.
We've seen them float to the surface
bloated—almost untouchable—
We've seen them face to face;
with puffed out-cheeks
as we bend over.

Devil Design

Devil design in the dell:
where there were trees
there are tires
treadless and moldering
fecal matter not drying
flies scavenging.
They fail themselves; they die.

Devil design up the hill:
where sheep did graze
so lovely, spikes
with a little stubble
grow.

Devil design down the road
stones blur, dirt blurs—
the road itself smiles:
"I'm out of here."

Where there was water
and war memories, circa 1920,
the poets exploded;
now the spikes grow tall
and thirsty
and no one reads.

The tree frog says,
I don't know where my health is.
I suspect it's in me now
and in my webs
but where is it really,
my health?

Devil design, moving about,
come to the veins,
has become the veins.

Failure

When we fail to grind our grimness,
our bitterness, down to dust,
we fail to foster the gleam
that brightens the year of a child's mind.

See us forlorn and bowed
hard-bitten as if on coal—
with a blackened tongue;
a tired will adrift—
compound an even greater loss

than shingle sucked back to sea
the sea wall weakened and cracked
the harbor too afloat, unmoored
and all the flowers—their roots
and stems—fast concluded in a bed of salt.

After the fall, on account of error,
we might rise like the old bird
up and out of folly—high flyers
spewing anger on dissolved winds,
hopeful souls bent on the hour's distraction.

Peach Pie

So there it is—
A peach pie on a platter
which will poison no one
who lives—thrives
under the nail of my right thumb

The treat is large & small & tasty
enough for all of us.
Yes—I keep my cuticles clean
& never raise my voice.

Holidays—not all of them—
I push my thumbnail up
gently
& release my friends
comfortably housed all this while.
We exercise together,
then I sit at & they on the table
face to face & we dine
and after the kind of conversation
that won't kill us either,
we feast on pie

peach pie

and the clouds roll off to sea
all fluffy and the blue sky

licking our lips and so forth

Another Salesman

Have I got a deal for you!
Look at that ocean—
400 acres plus and all the fathoms
your land-bound brain can conjure.
But don't mess with the fish.

With this wet province you save
on insurance.
But don't touch the fish.
Leave 'em alone. We want them safe.
Enjoy the sea,
it's new on the market.
As oceans go, this is quality.
Move quickly—there are well-heeled others
waiting in the wings.

Down South the deep lots
are being subdivided
and the fish are aware and going crazy.
They feel the heavy bidding
so they bite, accelerate—
many leave their schools.

It's a populous world for sale;
all bright colors beneath—forest and fish
and the surface is never the same
once you learn how to watch.
You'll watch all right:
the storms after such calms that rest you
will turn your watching into knowing,
better than owning a pasture in flood-time.
The billowy deep is miraculous—
I won't boost the obvious.
Listen—you can charge tolls,

income property;
you and your fortune will rise with the tides.
No one's going to move the moon.
But if you mess with the fish
the sea goes back to its owner,
the bank, of course, and honest folks,
the shareholders.

Father at 85

rails against his lapsed memory,
kicks against the gaps—
what was it he meant to be doing—
a missed cue in the talk-fest,
a slack look felt on his face
as it dulls.

Why does he worry his memory so
when most conceived in 1912
recall nothing—zero
they're colder than gone
more gone than the grave
stone—the lettering already fading
as in weathering;

and he's seen it happen over and again
in the fraught elongation of his years:
all the younger brothers gone before him
the wife of lifetimes gone before him
a young nephew and all those cousins
gone before him;

still, out of the stew he is
of grief and good fortune,
the griping goes on
—even over the olfactory,
the loss of the sense, he says,
except when some stench
sends it back to life, quivering.

My father's years are circles
around my circles.
He's there too in the rich plenitude
of his life; still a presence at the table,
alert and reaching over, demanding more.
He still wants more.

Jessie Beforehand

She's on the way to infantile,
a little sleep before the fitful rhythms.
A she, we know from the tests taken,
swims in the famous lucidity
of mother's love and our confusion.

Hop up—
with a dash and a caper!
Oh—the new jokes will come along,
a new tongue for new occasions.

We hang in the wings
a few feet back,
she'll have stepping space soon
and air, and weather conditions.

Tony's World

Barry Wallenstein

Tony Upbraids Himself

Tony—you're a slick/sick mutha-hubba
money in your ears
& your eyes are seeing halves—half
what the gold, so-called, is
worth

you think some god reached in your pocket
to teach you a lesson
make you go on less/less than half
& minus the loss

Tony, do you know how to minus?
We know—the whole world knows—
Canada, India, Brooklyn

look at your plate—what's there and
lick your lips and smile—in a minute
your face might be frozen,
or cold, Tony, cold

you know how to plus
so what add onto yourself what?
silks, pure wools—cashmere
left in the rain—
it's all the same

you're a dull toad, Tony
in a left-over stew;
you've stopped reading the news
'cause it's bad—even the comics are sad

wake up!

Tony Takes a Hammer to His Head

and doesn't miss.

Sadness in the shower room
and no one's there.
It's steamy.

But Tony's ok, still stirs
and is grateful.
He dresses well
and covers the cut.

The same hand that raised the tool
and let it go
now pencils the moustache thin
and rubs the creases from his clothes.

Why ever did he do it?
He says the curse came flying
and he pulled it down.

His arm is an agent.
His hand is an agent.
He needs a new agent.

Tony's Blade

Blade imagines it has memories
(sad blade, so delusional).
Its hesitation, shyness, on the table
signals nothing.   Or mind
has moved it that way.

Blade is without conscience
riding beneath the table's edge—
no glint—
more shadow there than flash.

It slides easily
along an angerless morning.
It never propels the hand.
It knows the natures of string,
of apple, and peach,
and the stuck lock.

The neighbor's tires are safe
not for slashing,
but, to tell the truth,
some days blade needs sharpening.

Tony's Head

Tony reads the news
smokes a joint
bites his lip, spins
and goes out to see the stylist
to have his hair turned red.

It's about time
his inner voice sings.
Why so dull for so long?

Walking with a new head
within the city's tendrils,
he's a bobbing red flame,
an aspect; electric boots and
a belt that shines have him flying.

In all this
Tony forgets what he's read:
the left hand column of print
fades to blue;
the right hand column
too fades to blue.

But a memory on page 7
holds him like a damp finger
on fresh ice.
Images of waste unconfuse—briefly:
nuclear mountains in the suburbs,
waves of poison overflowing
his stash; even his charm, obscured
by the images, cold and funny
as Death.

Smoke drifts from around the corner
lifting Tony slightly
wafting him home.

Tony's Preferences

Some prefer berries in cream
quiet music above
and a good book
open to a page that pleases the mind
while not dulling the taste for the berries
or the cream.

Myself, I prefer the brothel
on the east corner of Vine Street
over all the others
and for the ordinary reasons—the rose tints,
the skirts generally,
the scented space and tact of the staff—
how magically they appear with favors
and then disappear fast,
the breeze that comes off an evening
as sweetly as Suzie, Suzie from the alley,
slips out of very little and is delicate,
and then, best of all, she's not delicate
& hills,
yes, fresh as plump and the valleys

and the comfort comes home
in this place—years away from certainties
and the lustings after war.

Tony the City Booster

It's swell, this development down
Devil Design,
a street named for its goings on
near Joy St.—
down where Joy meets Flurry
near the harbor.
This is a fantastic old city

fallen behind the times maybe,
what with cracks widening
and time itself a burden
on the bridges and tunnels.
The way kids throw stones at each other
sometimes reminds me of unnatural decay:
simpering disrespect by the grown-ups
towards their own kind too,
gives me gas; it's all the same & wearying.

But now on Devil Design St.
three shops from the corner
where stood two houses till they fell,
a field has been allowed to take
with trees and a hill on the south side
looking over the boats,
towards, some days, the sunset.

This spot of country in the city
hasn't slowed down the trading
or the circular dancing.
If someone's to be cut or rewarded,
it still happens here on one of those
end of the century streets.

Little Bestiary

I'm not in love with Tony
said the snake to the frog
and the frog said really (?)
look at yourself curled about yourself
like a hose on a wheel.

Snake says it's something else,
—symbiosis; he's a symbol:
sex but not love.

He knows I'm harmless
but my movement amazes him.
He steps back from my slither.

He may be taller than the average
man. I can't tell and
from this height it doesn't matter.

It does says the frog—
everything does, especially his nature.
This guy, Tony,
for all his skill at bending over,
is unsure of animals.
His touch is the tentative kind, I know.

Shisssssss, says the snake
his touch on you is all you know.
His nature is in place,
let's hope his heart keeps beating.

Tony to His Mother

Sad news—new charges on the way
& they're false & near
and you lie there, under lid
these five years.
I won't obey
or listen to rumors.

Mother, if you can see me,
imagine a well-carpeted iceberg,
thick enough for an eight day week.
And I'm alone on it
in a very comfortable chair—
a Morris design.
And we're drifting out to sea,
the berg, its luxuries and me.

Mother, imagine it sailing way out
and me getting smaller and smaller,
a familiar shape fading to a blur;
but you'll know—
always, your quiet, stern knowing—
that I'm small, diminishing
only from where you're sitting,
and you'll know too, I'm relatively safe.

Tony's Dad

carried him across a river of blood.

The fat in the slaughterhouse,
in the stone room
adjacent to the killing rooms,
would clog in the drain
and the steers' blood puddled
high enough for a young Tony
to need either hip boots
or a lift onto father's difficult shoulders.

Tony loves to tell the story:
"As a small boy I hugged a white butcher's coat
blotted red. By the end of the day
slick and greasy, more red than white
already, during the ride, foul and smelly
and I was right in it, almost joyful
and afraid especially of the butchers' eyes
as they turned from the knives and hooks
to my position on the boss's back.

"He was their boss
not mine exactly, but
blame him not now for my imagination
then about bosses and papas and
different kinds of muscle than my own.
And what did I own really,
other than the lift and carry?

"They bled the cattle
but clubbed the calves—
all to do with the taste of the meat
and young as I was, I studied it."

Tony Cleans the Stove

Some hooks the mind comes up with
endanger the mind itself,
so I blunt the points,
file down the barbs
and find great pleasure in cleaning the stove:
scouring powder and the pink sponge,
the whole arm tightening
bearing down on a fast scrub,
the black crust softening to be gone
and—it always happens—
the gleam appears beneath my hand
having waited the whole day to shine.

I've seen a member of my tribe
more than once turn a two into a twenty—
she's the one famous
for the step out into the hall,
the cigarette break, and the two hour doze
in the middle of a skirmish.
Yet she does that one sly trick,
the two into twenty.
Its very meagerness smacks of vanity.

I'd rather go back to the stove.

Tony Practices

being awake
not just eyes open and steady
but on the mark
get ready and should
gun go pop, go fast
as if fleet foot
the famous hound from hell
were panting down the path.

He practices
bob and weave
to skirt the corners
of tiny dooms
and the larger unspeakable errors.

He also practices threading needles
in breezy weather
and then he practices deeper
sewing split seams on a skirt
of someone
to gain her favor—
he mends the damage
on item after item in her drawer.

He practices greeting her
before she arrives.
He opens his arms and everything.
He does it everywhere excepting
in front of the mirror,
and when she arrives
sweaty after *her* run,
he practices further
with greater concentration.

Tony Visits Hotel Splendide

After a week with my arms
around very little—
nothing really to talk about
after my pet spider quit being a spider,
I had a will to splurge—
moved into the Hotel Splendide.

The drinks at the lounge bar
need neither mixer nor chaser,
tipping back and getting the glad-eye.
Conversation too goes down like rain
with faces moving in, personal
in the middle of time off at the Hotel Splendide.

Speaking with a person named Randy,
I remembered how ill I'd felt one time
running to meet another Randy,
falling down on my way.
The current Randy is my feel-better mate
lately met and smiling at the Hotel Splendide.

Another character, call him Joe,
told me about his wife of some 30 years
and how his travels divided him,
sometimes quartered him—but he
never lost his memory,
stopping off at the Hotel Splendide.

They say if you stay a week
and no one dies at the Hotel Splendide
and the topic itself never comes up,
chances are you'll stay longer
and lose your watchfulness,
your bitterness.

Myself, I scan the daily papers now,
study first the box scores
then the obituaries.
There's the need to know
who's won and lost
off the grounds of Hotel Splendide.

Who wouldn't give up false love
or the dream of being that way loved,
for needed facts that can't be fudged?
Hotel Splendide, come by on a whim,
gave me armfuls and respite—
not cold truths; I'm on my way home.

The Day of Withholding

After years of forestalling the dream,
the dream arrived:
Tony asked for a shirt and it was not given
he asked for a hat and it was withheld
he asked for some extra time and that too was denied

even kind words, previously on time,
coalesced into NO—
the violent negation and silence—
nor was the safety pin handed over;
and the shirt that was once his went unreturned.

Oh, sweet miracle of dream—
to not miss what was not given!

Tony's dream:
on the day of withholding, his cart wheeled as easily—
uphill as on the level or down,
and being smart, he read the dream as
a clue to a cleaner slate.

He went along a dozen days without,
and on the night of that 12th day,
concerned about the number 13,
he smacked his lips and feasted.

Tony to His Creator

Someone else in my voice—
it's frightening
worse than a bone caught
& a choke

I feel my pulse slowing
& now, again, speeding

Who's in the wings?

Is what I say His echo
or does He simply—even when softly—
speak through me
as if I were His dummy
His screen, scrim, sieve—
megaphone, finally
blasting His message
that Tony's a walker, a skipper
& a jumper—toss him in water
he'll swim—knock him down—
he'll take a nap

Whoever is out there presses me daily

No matter the pressure, I'm talking!
While the Grand Old Master
fumbles for a stick, anything—
to write His own story.

That was Then; Now is Paid For

Novocain Mary, lately out of stir,
balances on a bed's edge
and ponders the ways to rise.
Once vertical though listing, she slips from the room
and into the luxury of Handsome Harry—

his white, fully loaded, hand washed
four door Cadillac—1980s something—
faux leopard seat cushions
stereo surround sound and a sunroof
made of bomb-proof glass—real glass—

Harry turns the silver key
a smooth click and a hum—
the quietest sound in silverdom.
They sail through the city;
with the clock on the dash on time.

In the bath sometimes Mary encouraged a toy boat
to float in her direction.
She smiles at the recollection of her pleasures,
and watches expectantly as Harry drives the car
into the outer boroughs.

As Per Intent

It was around 5 a.m.,
in an uptown section of Toledo,
when the blade made its way—
no, plunged through Antonio's heart
where it stopped and started to melt,
the blood thinning out to rivulets
welling into pools.

The shaft was the last to liquefy
and by then the pools were still enough
to hold the flickering lights
from the many candles set about.

So, as per intent, Antonio passed away
while the murderer slipped away,
his hands already drying,
in the direction of Hotel Bye-N-Bye,
where in the back of the kitchen
he'll sculpt ice into angels for weddings,
and atop his fancy, a frosty delight:
tiny brides and grooms with fearless faces.

New Poems: Drastic Dislocations

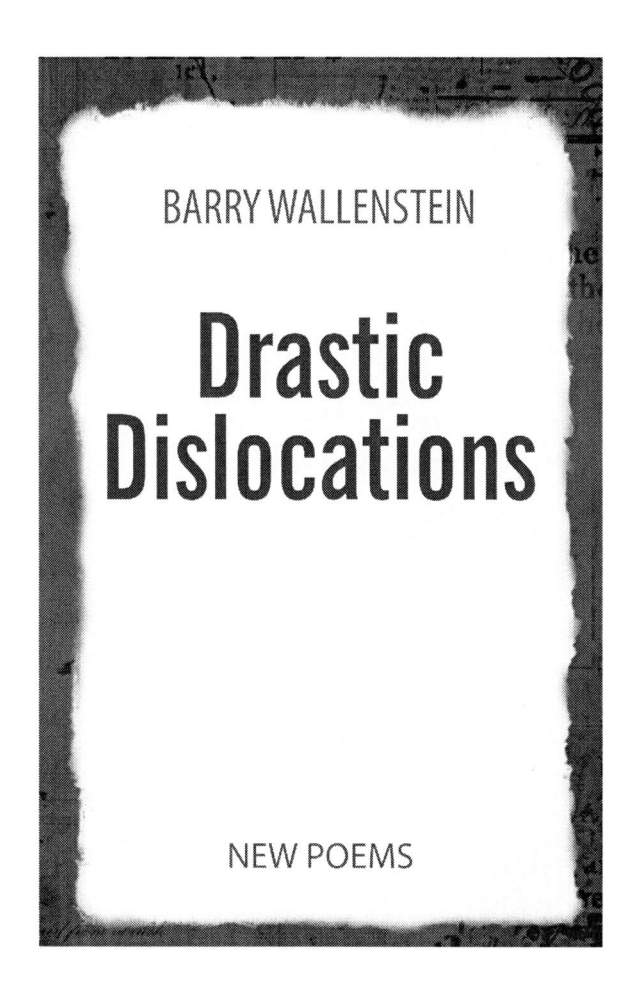

1. Euphoria Ripens

The Fabulous Backdrop

On this night, one storm having passed
and the night sky cool with starlight
and moonlight planting shadows
against the giant hills, the birds are all but still;
and the rustlings in the leaves
are becoming whispers,
while a breeze kissed by honeysuckle
carries off the daytime armor.

The nuzzlings going on in caves and warrens
are innocent—but before this night is over,
a creature will call out in heaven-piercing pain
waking up to the present moment.
Lambs hurry, all woolly and yielding,
to lie down with wolf cubs restless and teething.

Under the Branches

Two old men talk of suspenders
under a single branch.

Two girls lazily talk of boys
underneath a single branch.

Two young out-and-abouts fool around;
one jumps up to touch a branch.

Two sweet peas beneath a branch,
each one waiting for a taste.

Two notes sounded by the hand
of an artist sitting below a branch.

Two ideas placed in a basket
under a branch; one pops up and sings.

Two clocks tick as summer revelers
dance in the shadows of the branch.

In late autumn, during a storm,
some branches fall to the ground

to be gathered by groups of two,
bundled up, their arms like branches,
and carried off for kindling.

The Bullhorn

Death the bullhorn blows its name
beyond the hills, or the thought of hills,
beyond the soup kitchens, the picnics,
the summer days that last forever,
beyond distances that skirt the mind
and cannot be reckoned.

But Death the big-shot, the capital D
even in the middle of a line,
hasn't been fast enough or thorough enough
for the breathers have outstripped the breathless;
more folk talking this day
than all the ghosts in history.

Death, what could be more predictable
than the spell you put on a town
at bombing time
or the closing of anyone's eyes?
We all know the shape of your hood,
the measured pace of your lengthening stride.

Yet in the face of Death,
whether it come to neighbor, cousin,
friend—even to the enemy,
we feign surprise, as if that
which happens more easily than rain,
were both an outrage and original.

No wonder aliens from outer space
delight, confuse us, as they fly
independent of your rules,
Death, you regular thing,
all that silence and silencing.

Commitment to a Fog

for Jean-Jacques Boin

as it rolls in on a downdraft
and settles in the nooks and flats
of the lower hills, their green saddles, and then
comes that slow spilling into the gorge-rent valley.

One could inhale such fog
and be healthier for it;

I mean, to paraphrase the man tied up for his own good,
my mind is fog-bound, the foreground's enshrined
and the background is all pastel under a spell of gray:
no telling if they're houses out there or foggy notions.

I've inhaled the better part
of a year of fog and that might be a decade.

I mean, in the language of fog,
the indistinct seems particular
and all the dead—so bright and sharp, so clear-headed,
so loved in their lifetimes, are caught again in my fog
as if I'd given them my condition.

Sounds Above the Monastery

The cock's crow—the sound
coming down the hill on a still morning—
signifies, as does the donkey's bray,
the bleating sounds, the buzzing sounds,
blathering sounds—a man passing deliberately
scraping against the pavement—
passing wind.

A young woman sings alone
in the terraced garden sitting in the sunshine.
Listen to the far off bell
hanging from the strong neck of the ass—
faint behind the voice.

The audible moths tap up against the window;
puck puck—they count too—always shedding their powder.

The Nightmare

The monster reaches out of the bog:
grave is the monster and foul the fog.
With hoary arms, gnarled hands
and flared nostrils, the threat lunges,
and the action is unrelated to love.

In my sleep I feel the fear ascending,
but I blink back the danger
and peer into my hand;
in my sleep I investigate my palm:
the creases are a merciful find.

Just yards from the bog with its images
and sinking notions
are the fertile downs,
but the threatening truths on fire
hiss in the trap of the dream.

Shades of Keats

The cicadas are amorous tonight
in the realm of our listening.
How should we behave under such sound,
the waves of it teasing our minds
out of thought? Keatsian trills thrill down
to the exposed nerve beneath a broken tooth.

Is that anger I now hear
within the singing insects' song,
or is some creature resisting penetration?
Are we truly one or are we two?
This is the rasp I hear
against a fallen heaven.

Waters rise somewhere in a flood
only to recede while others ascend.
These facts are registered in the music made
on the creature's tymbal organ.
Why so sexy, the lovers wonder,
leaning close, trying to understand, listening.

Do the Dead?

Do the dead assume the same age?
Fresh arrivals and old timers—
all the ghosts—chattering the same way,
bent over the same way and drifting,
all wearing each other's fame?
I'd like to guess yes—
Death, the democratic ideal,
an even line dissolving time.

The smart money says no,
and I see myself soon lost
within the group of young departed,
not knowing where to sit or whom to talk to;
but then there's the lift, the flash of reverence,
my eyes climbing the ladder toward the old ones,
the Greeks and the Hebrews—
that towering wisdom and calm in their eyes—
and it's paradise.

His Precarious Mood

The boy, feeling that way,
strips the bark off two sticks,
rubs them smooth for the oil and the color,
then slants them slightly
to balance against a knee.

Positioned that way
he imagines gaining significance—
displaying a way of handling
and assembling with care while listening –
he calls it a start in the direction
of significance.

Eventually bleachers are erected
and a stadium rises.
The lights, the eyes, train on the boy
while he adjusts his sticks
in the broken shadow of a ladder.

So many climb up to watch,
feeling significance arriving,
when suddenly the boy sweeps aside
the balanced twigs and starts anew
with a deck of cards—a penthouse of aces,
and the clubs, diamonds, hearts, and spades
zigzag up the ascending magic.

A draft stirs the stadium
challenging the walls tilted on their edges;
but the house of cards
well made and braced by luck
doesn't quiver, lean, or fall.

Grains of Sand

1.

Euphoria Ripens

For all who luxuriate in
time's slow drag,
there are others who alertly watch
the joys and sorrows
of one man passing into another man's jaw.

Here in counting country,
those who line up with the half time,
slow time tickers
are lollygagging yet proud,
while the rest of us go click click click
our bodies hurling forward
toward the wheel.

Every morning on every leaf
the dews gather;
they bubble and shine in the rising sun;
slowly, then quickly they dry.

2.

Grains of Sand

A wizened man is bent under the skyway
muttering questions. He's located
somewhere north of the equator
and south of Finland,
in the middle of clover and soft mosses.

He calls Lady Time a mute witch, fanciful
and indifferent to digits.
She discounts clocks, he says, and abilities.
Does she know the roots of inquiry, he inquires
and quavers before her skirts.

The tense of a lifetime slips past its mooring.
Jabber what what what into the reckoning.

3.

Mortality

The murmur of an infant
prompts me to check my watch
again and again, but I resist.

Same thing at 6 months,
at 2, and again, I remember,
at 4, 5, 6...
all the lasting digits.

I listen closely
but don't keep time,
while you, clown under a hood
with the surety of scythe,
persist in the counting.

4.

October 24th 2009: Daylight Savings Time

The gift of an hour this day
is, I've heard it said,
something just off the shoulder
of a blessing—something sweet and slow;
yet that gift, this extra,
confounds the moments
between now and November,

after which time the quotidian
will rub the board blank, and we'll hear
some powerful voice from out of a tree,
bellow:
"it's twelve o'clock all over the world—
the time is set and always has been;
my name is inscribed beneath your skin."

Items of the Grave

This man, near to his end,
glimpses the rise up ahead
and cries out: all this must go down—
the clean suit they'll dress the thing in
pockets empty of cash
the botched memory—
the failure to spell in any language
the chipped tooth just off center
the deformed arthritic fourth finger
on the left hand clenched—
the fear of losing—
gold and silver fillings too,
let them go and the fear of falling—
let that drop with weight—
fresh soil on it;
bury the scorn—the unreason
and the idea of dates in time—
shove them well under.
Entomb the vain rational.

Minus a Wheelbarrow

So little depends
upon

the witty phrase
delivered

by the mouths of
critics

stunned by the
wrinkle

in Death's dark
brow.

"Lifey/Deathy": Sewer and Tree

1.

You empty your bladder
& you purge your bowels,
you empty, you purge,
empty, purge.
Then one dark night
luminous flash near its height
you stop—
the years of letting it go
have gone
all that shittin' and pissin'
down the drain.

2.

But there's love:
the boy by the cherry tree
picking lightly at the reddish bark
imagines carving a heart
with an arrow in it
and a name he loves to spell,
but some qualm about
caging her name in wood
drives the boy to drop his knife.
Then, he shouts her name to the air
where the echo lasts no longer
than a lilac's breath.

The Old Man

From his watery eyes
to his pudding knees,
the old man
is not—has long been not—
a rubber ball in the hands of
that boy or that girl.

He is not a funeral
nor, at this time of evening,
is he a wedding—
the guests jolly cavorting,
forgetting everything.

Soldiers in the distance, stand watch
as the village sleeps;
the young men snooze in their lovers' arms.
He is not yet debris, piling
miles from the playground.

His brain is grey as a baby's pink;
it flashes, still healthy,
travels faster than the boy's pitch
or the girl's laughter.
Listen: the mind sounds like an arrow,
it sounds like an ocean.
He tastes the salt in the air.

The Excesses of Advancing Age

At the end of the day,
he took better care of his breath
than his breathing—a deep imbiber—
executive sessions with leftover bottles—
gin generally.

Before all that
he worried a bald spot
until it became an area,
and then a plain
barren with nothing to graze on.

And then he took to smoking
factory products
and weed from the garden too—
a slow smoker, a deep toker
a fool along the measuring rope of time.

Toward the end of the day,
he fell in love with a piece of sugar,
a little soil on the side,
and an off the chart IQ.
They never quarreled
and made love beyond the law.

What's left of his memory
never forgets her
and the surprise—every time.

Paradise Lane

To the left of the stump
where the five branches bloomed
—until blight brought them down—
is a small street called Paradise Lane.

This path defies retribution
as it weaves and narrows forever.
People walk there arm in arm, well-dressed,
an intermittent diamond among them.

With cautious chit chat and the clearing of throats,
handsome bodies and abundant nature,
the lane itself slips around its name
as easily as a child runs into a cave

Prayer

Nature out there—great fire-breather
mother of the toad and the gorgeous hunk

lead and gold and all that glows;

stirrer of storms, floodtide, lava flow—
please out there

don't take away my stumbling block;
leave alone my stumbling block
and if there's a storm, let it come down!

2. Drastic Dislocations

Pandemonium

They, driven by doubt and a whim, opened the box
and out everything jumped, fluorescent

and fearsome, and the box became famous
for its nightclub/late nighttime release and later

worse, that rumble before the joists gave
and the bleeding call to the world,

but the world wasn't listening
with its nations pinpoint pressed to the wall;

the nations' armies slouch in lassitude and fog
while the generals speed to their offices

to measure out the scores of blame,
long having forgotten the box and its many tongues of flame.

The Job

Sometimes this air I'm in
is so sulfurous, thick and unworthy,
I need to take much shorter breaths
to widen the zone of gasping.

My odd job is
to remember and write down,
with pencil not pen,
the names of the ones disappeared,
then I hand the papers back
to the state.

I'm not very good at this
and soon expect a reprimand.
I confuse Joe with Josephine,
Michael with Michelle,
Sally with Sally—gender errors.
And, on occasion, I reverse the truths
of their expirations.

Stupid me.
They all went quickly I report.
The few lawsuits die in court.
When the air is really bad
we all lean westward
and curse our jobs.

But if I lose this assignment
I may have to be pushing buttons again,
as during that sorrowful time
melting by the Equator,
counting children;
that was not a job to talk about.

Serving the State

Under the sway of perfidy's rule
the sleepers awake,
soon to do as they've done before,
cut into the cells of the state—
where they curl again
to do their sleeping thing.

The state of my mind:
I mind the store
—dry goods, lemons,
anything that bites the tongue
or profits.

My rat's pulse
my toad's liver
my skinny skeletal whole self
is on everyone's side plus my own.

Sleep and scratch I do
and down I drown, cell-bound,
into the brackish waters
where the sleepers awake,
as they do on dry land,
thrashing.

I'm the accompanist.

Days of the Week

*Monday is not a plot
but a beginning—*

Monday ordinarily implies Tuesday;
in plague times, it is a beautiful word, a wish.
At any time, without Tuesday
Monday would be a large hall holding
a small voice depending on echoes,

so there *is* Tuesday, and no matter how challenging,
how bloody or relaxing, Wednesday follows
like an athlete in full stride towards

Thursday—the excitement of long nights
a couple of days away and a chance for
yearning ahead, heading into

Friday—where the eagles fly far away from gray.
Someone's going to buy a round or two, and
everything will be red and gentle and spilling to

Saturday Sunday the Weekend
and let's get lost
or lustily enjoy bed and board—
slipping from outfits, too fashionable.

But should madness leap its boundary
and Monday indeed not be followed
by all those lovely names that end in day,
then let that Monday be the lengthy kind
with its seconds ticking like hours and
each hour replicating an eon
and sleep just an idea entertained by the waking.

Baggage

Lately it's all silly baggage
foolish rumination:
imagine—putting the carpet down
for an agile teen,
helping a worm navigate the loam,
arranging the day
according to the lord's privilege
whose need is appalling, anyway, and
silly,
and that sound suggests a world of stumbling,

everyone buckling down
to solve first one oh-so-personal problem
and then a second.

The poets have strayed over the hill
their sad songs trembling only grasses.

The judge, loathing the bench, smiles and convicts.
Men in stripes horse around in the stone yard,

while the poets' far-off strains are unheard—
error & folly
no one left to step the rhythm down.

A small bomb floats out of the sky—
a lonely piece of confetti.
A compass guides it down
to the middle of the party
where cities and their populations
enjoy food and company.
Which fool said it had to come down?

Drastic Dislocations

He's alive, but barely;
the fall from space
was a long way down
and the sound of the impact
astounding.

It's a miracle really
to see/hear him breathing, even sighing
out of his twisted parts
and drastic dislocations.
—he sighs, they say, for us all—

No blood.
The mystery of his flight and landing
is taking attention off the war,
and has drawn the world to wonder:
Who goes there? What's the look?

TV crews, foreign and domestic, circle the amazement,
set up camp; food and drink are flown in,
enough to keep us full and salty for a year,
enough to take our minds off the boxes stacking,
while this fellow, out of nowhere, extenuates his sighing.

Distant Music

The sun alone is not scorching the day,
though the grasses are brown
the ditches dry
and all my dizzy wishes fizzle in the glare.

The distant sparrow's wings are signaling;
widows carry fewer items to the bureau drawer;
jackhammers stop and then continue as before.

The music heard faintly a week ago—
was it a horn or a voice
filtering through the woods—has stopped.
Instead there is a metallic noise,
a sound of a sledge striking an anvil.
Over the hill wood is scraping against itself;
there's that churning again and the siren.

Waters Rising

1.
The Rain

The rain was general all over the Northeast
and heavy all through the first week of broadcasts.
At first we welcomed the cleansing,
all that dirt rushing down the drains,
and a fine excuse for remaining indoors—
playing Civilization and making small boats.

During the second week, perhaps caught in a wind trap,
the rain held up and seemed about to stop
but then revved up its engine, came on strong.
By the end of that week,
the damp had found its way into our pockets,
our folded money stuck and worthless.

At the end of a solid month,
the raindrops, caught in an endless spell,
became larger and larger with
flecks inside huge enough to study
—actual sunsets over cities and
combinations drying on suburban lines.

The raindrops look better each day:
rain against white; rain against black,
everything shines outward.

2.
Gazing at Raindrops

Here's a raindrop large as a globe;
inside are three giant glaciers floating south—
cities being rubbed and jostled by the flow,
and the smaller islands have gone under
to sand bars. Only the old maps
show the earlier story: picturesque.

The raindrop on its right reveals the mountains;
Tarzan is seen smiling—
swinging from a tree.
The others have stripped to their shorts and
are waving their fisted hands heavenward
as the waters rise relentlessly.

The raindrop to the left is even larger
and the performances within are wild:
a fevered auto race with Silver Streak in the lead,
and above that, as the hill rises and crests,
a fair with a Ferris wheel is in progress
and the children shriek high above everything.

They are dry. The hero in the tree is dry.
Only those in cities—always built on waterways,
always in need of channels—
are scurrying about.
The automobiles and trains are under water,
and the boat builders rush to their craft.

When the raindrops pop and dry,
as they will in the returning sunlight,
all that was seen inside them
will be gone with the drops.

The Subject

Shadows on a clock;
a donkey brays on the upper field.

The subject slides under the rug
—not as if swept there—
rather, the subject's ebullient life
drove it in that direction.
It's a bulge now;
press it down repeatedly
and it reappears in a different shape,
a cow or a bull, let's say,
just at the carpet's edge.
Anyone could bend over and gather it up
but not the whole business.
Some bits might cling beneath the rug,
enough for a poem,
enough gas to get to the next pump.

Shadows flick against the window;
the braying carries on all night.

Cleansing Ritual

See the crowd gathering
around the preacher,
clamoring for his blood—
the day before he's to leave town
on account of some serious lapse,
a shame on himself and his following.

It seems he paid too little
for some pleasure thing,
with someone else watching—
wet lips and all.
Two scoundrels inflicting one pain
and only one's to pay.

Something went wrong—
the original price misunderstood,
a careless word overheard
by a true believer waiting for a chance,
catching a whiff, in collusion with a heaven
disinclined towards original sin.

The Killers Again

The boy, now a man,
raised on barbed wire avenues
of lonely city # 3
or blasted city # 4—
worked himself bloody-handed
out of one flat into a larger one
curtains and flatware
and then to a suburban house
drapes and china
and then a larger one with a yard
and a boat up on blocks
and so on up the ladder of corpses
and each time now
his hands are cleaner.

Omit the acts of grace
that hide in mortuary pockets
and risk the distance place to place.

Anger, a Personal History

He takes a sip from his arm
and thinks it's gin
cramps soon after and a head full of woe.

His doctor says two shots a day
ok but the third will kill you;
Anger tips back four and pats its lips.

He fumbles along a tricky lane
as dangerously weedy
as the wish to stumble—fool!

Bite down and wince—lack-brain
he is—hooks and spikes
all set inward and rusting.

Its sweet caress grates along his spine.

3. *Lorelei*

What's Now

She didn't think she'd love it
just that way and so very much
and in view of the others, but she did
and then demanded—
in a feathery, slowly halting
but clear voice—
that the performance be extended
beyond the original hour and intention
and that what's now last forever
but with time-spaces in which to travel
to India, to Asia,
to the deep and humid South.

"We could take what's now and stage it
before a small group of friends at first
and then maybe at a club
triangular tables—mirrored tops—
three chairs per table;
and the onlookers, silent and restrained,
would remain dressed for such a club
always,"

and should someone call out "swamp girl,
sale bête," she'd hear nothing but
the band playing in the background
and her heart's rhythmic pounding.
She'd know—every touch from childhood on
has told her so—that this moment now,
rippling beyond borders,
might prove her very best chance.

Lorelei

Cast a different set of dice
—direction Lorelei—
an island of spices
a package tight as Lorelei

sprung from a dream
and a good luck toss—
this straight-backed head high
visage of Lorelei.

In earlier days the dice said:
love that tree for its knothole
the blades of grass for their fancy
and anything that moves without speaking.

Thus I shared the loneliness of the grass,
the shame of the tree,
and rolled again till the bones came yes
the swift gait and swaying—Lorelei ascending.

Bending, she blows on the sand—golden to the eye
and a cloud goes up shape shifting—breath of Lorelei.

The Invitation

I've a bed as large as a yard,
you could hang loose and pick your corner

The pillow is goose-down
with a hill and a gorge

Should my breathing be a bother
you could blend in with the bushes

startle the birds from their nests
or wait for me to stop

This bed is a glory thing
large love and brimming

Come into my yard
sweet person

with your eyes wild,
I mean darting, and wise.

Lost

If I were lost in that waiting tunnel,
the one to the left of the spiral,
or caught trapped in a major cloud,
would you find me
—cut through wool
and bathe me as you did those days in Cleveland?

My guess today is no,
because there was a time
10 days ago and another just 3 days past,
when I was missing—even from myself,
and you, a whirling dervish,
your mind in concert with your body,
did not send out small spurs,
the ones that could hook what's left of me—
a little fish almost, with my lips pursed
swimming in a great dark sea.

Letter to My Daughter

Dear Jessie:

Remember, just before the rainstorm
up the street came the hurdy-gurdy—
colorful as colorful is
with a small gray monkey
grinding a red organ.
The handle was brass
and he—the monkey was a he—
wore orange gloves,
his tin cup clinking the coins
given by merry makers on that day.

Remember too,
during the flood tides
prior to recognition—
and you will recognize
everything—
there will be a dry place
for you to slip into
that will feel like years,
will be like entering the kingdom of Fact
with noise and congratulations.

Remember, right after,
when you recall that citadel
of vaulted ceilings and views
of rising waters out of prismed windows,
you were never in danger, my daughter.
That little monkey and his friend,
the hurdy-gurdy man, has eyes
of protective power—besides,
you move too quickly for danger.

The Diamond Dealer's Lament

At 3 am she's a drench of tears
and her crying swamps
the angel hours of our night
and challenges my attention
to this perfect diamond
resting on a square of black velvet.

These are the longest hours,
the anxious times
before age advances
to alter such wild misery
and her tantrum's sway.

I've left my minor fascination
and my employment hours ago.
Shadows fall on the loupe,
the tweezers—all the trappings
of my trade.

She squeezes her eyes shut,
her mouth an oval of noise,
a wise dissonance.
I don't relax into those sounds
or desire balance, or any sweet equanimity.

The round world is riotous,
a few markets rise in the rampant fall,
while the generations are sleeping,
soon to be measured against the sounds
of my daughter's weeping.

Lover

Rabbits run to rabbit's care,
paw to paw crease to crease,
while you annihilate my sullen moods
and lead me to my animal side—
I burrow in furrows
for the salty glide,
clamber up tree trunks
for the succulent reds,
trace the marks where your rhythm tread.

So it goes and well into winter,
a tiger in town and me a twister,
a sweet-toothed monster
in love with a dancer and, at times,
her rising pulse. Slow me down—
I mean yes, if you need to—
and I'll fall in step with your rhythm if I can,
but put down your fan, your grip on the duende,
read my verses and hold my hand.

Ballad

What are you doing my darling son?
I'm sitting in this boat, dear mother.

And where is your boat my son, pray tell?
At sea in the distance my mother.

You're breaking my heart dear child, fair boy
for you're lost I fear on the deep dark sea.

Lost I am but not from you
my handsome extravagant mother,

I am away at sea but my voice reaches out.
It calls out for you my mother.

I see what you're doing my son, she says.
I'm doing very little mother dear.

Then why has love left from the lines of your face
and why is your voice now retreating?

Because I'm lost at sea, cold and frightened I am
and I'm gone for sure my mother.

Old Friends

>   *for John Tytell*

could be like twins at ease,
but in this case,
the wealth is in a different fund.

Forty years wrap us around so tightly
that our differences,
sharper and more sprightly now,
are insulated by our bonds.

Over a thousand times we've met;
we've dined beneath raised voices,
yours the ebullient, the explosive,
mine a careful drive, a reticent caution.

After years of quarrelling and hand clasping,
we turn to each other again
having altered from boys to men,
young seniors with a company plan.

We study the menus well,
—keep our small world civil.

A Man

[1912—2005]

In 1926, my father drove through the city
via the transverse from west to east
sitting straight on a wooden cart
drawn by a horse.
There was a blizzard that day
and the way was slow
and the axle broke
and he fixed it with his hands—chafed and bleeding.

He's not famous for that,
but the story's told how he stole
the blanket off the horse to cover his legs.
He should be known as master of making do,
of making sure the done thing stayed.
He was a sticker
building a large pile out of nothing,
and he'd protect it with a hammer if needed.

There was no grand goal except to squeeze advantage
from the minute's allowance—to let the heap rise higher.
He took us to it scrambling along the way
and when we fell from weariness, he carried us there,
sat us down, kissed our eyes,
and told us how to be fond of fortune's excess.

Then this person of thunder
talked of friendship,
of competition—looking each man in the eye.

Ode

An old man's *shmekele*,
archetype of scorn,
sure coin for jesters,
can still be proud,
a swelled head and bursting,
and not just from memory,
though memories prevail:
the tireless plunges
into the bushes,
the roly-poly down the hill
and the dip into the pond.

When the pond's owner was out of town,
young *schmekele* just carried on,
rarely worrying if he had it right.
All the brightest moments,
even if they're distant,
no matter how they merge,
were led by this little man
and his funny life.

Its head recalls exposure and drafts,
the early cut, the fuss,
years of frenzy and distraction
and finally, a lame excuse.
Still, hope incandescent lives, *halevai*!
with the hint of indecency,
some careless words, a caress as of yore,
this relaxed member, this *pitzele shmekele*,
might, phoenix-like,
behave in a delighted manner,
confused again and defiantly unrelaxed;
any owner would be proud.

[*shmekele*=small penis; *halevai*=if only, god willing; *pitzele*=very small]

Inside Our Heads: Devil Design

The devil within my head does breeze
too fast for a kiss or a slaughter;
this neutered imp does prick and please.

Then he lingers and works his tease
to bind me to his lascivious daughter;
the devil plays in my head as a breeze.

He makes me bow to the world's dis-ease
jolly as a frog paddling water;
this neutered imp must prick and please.

I found her, touched her, now I grieve
down the slopes of this licentious daughter.
The devil within my head does freeze.

He holds us blind, maddened by degrees,
led by her wiles toward a funeral pyre,
this whelp with his prick and his please.

Love lies shunned by all lust's ease;
flames surround this craven lover.
The devil inside my head does breeze;
the more the imp does prick and please.

Sex Ghazal

He comes up from under into the garden of sex
with a cool soft cloth for after to calm his sex.

There are wizards and elves—harmless beings
dappled darlings delaying performance of sex.

Agony too lumbers its way onto a meadow:
frost and killer weeds spreading all their sex.

July heat in the city smokes up the horizon;
felines, long ago fixed, fitfully dream of lost sex.

There's a couple on the street casting glances
nothing more pure than party sex.

Autumn colors peak to fire then frizzle fast
as they dash to the terminus, the drying of their sex.

Enormous disputes issue from board rooms,
court rooms and where the warriors defile the sex.

Storms do come down—points of heat-lightning too;
dangerous swimming always in the sea swells of sex.

Bartering

I need lessons to learn your language
but with my funds on an outgoing tide—
flotsam in any language—
I propose a trade:

massage for language training.
After studying for the past five years
with a master masseuse,
the muscular Helga from Sweden,

I've become a master too:
I can unknot the spasmed shoulder,
remove the pain from the neck,
relax a frozen spine,

and make an old thigh feel young.
I employ only the best of oils—
eucalyptus modified by secret unguents;
the scent will send you to heaven.

Your language is a maze to me;
but in your voice I hear its music.
I want to master the tongue and
not settle for melodious impressions.

Let's try to understand each other
as best we're able;
all you need is a towel.
I'll bring the table.

I Think

a very large animal,
maybe a cousin of the tiger,
mistook the facade of my house
for a lover
and raked its claws across the front door,
the breast plate of my heart's seclusion.

I'm not frightened: this furry presence
stalks my house now
as if to keep it safe and
fixed to the ground
lest it drift upwards
to a dream neither he nor I desires.

The door was too fine anyway,
the stained glass a risky detail.
So we, the beast and I,
keep our eyes on level ground.
Should either of us glance over
we'd risk the chance of sullen recognition.

Llosa's Bad Girl

He sees her face circled
in a smoke ring of curls
sending out wisps—spun gold
destined for no merchant's shop.
He implores "please reach your arms
behind your waist please and
with your palms and fingers
treat slowly what you handle that way
and I'll kiss your eyelids open should they shut.
Shut might suggest sleep—a state
neither you nor I desire now or for a while."

And the next day everything's different;
he's lost in an office at work and Bad Girl
is far off in another office
in a different time zone
playing with friends or alone.
Good Boy picks up the phone
and calls the voice he needs to hear.
She asks him how he's dressed. He tells.
She describes how she's dressed. He smiles
and asks where her left hand lies
and she tells.

The Man Upstairs

flosses his teeth regularly
rinses well—dresses in a salmon-colored suit
with plush velvet on the wide lapels
no underwear no socks
alligator moccasins.

He keeps his secret behind a curtain
—a little balloon man—
perfect, rubber and silk;
the dummy's perfectly buck naked
a peach of a boy-man—pink flesh,
silent of course and affectless.
Some days he scolds his friend.
On account of the children,
he won't call anyone to watch.

When it's late at night, he lifts the curtain,
removes his suit and fancy shoes,
and addresses his prop, his company:
"Don't move you silly thing.
These last few weeks, any move
will upset my balance.
I've two kids to feed and educate
a job, a wife, and a mistress who's fine.
You could make me infamous for all time
and for all the wrong reasons. Stop it!"

The Circus Man

The carny barker boasts & cries—
"step right up folks…see in this tent
the world's strongest man alive,
and on the left stands the smallest woman,
a midget minus a half she is,
and see right in here folks, the famous geek,
feathers still on his lips
and there's the one who swallows knives
and then fire—
step right up folks / take it all in—my friends."

But in the shadows,
he groans to himself:
"I've lost a son, missing these many months
and in my own home town;
for me he's as far away as China.
He left soundlessly—first he's here
and then nothing, zero, silence.
He took his gear, his pipe and everything.
Some would smile at such a young man
smoking a pipe. He never smiled back.

I couldn't interest him in the animals
or the freaks—fascinations for most kids.
No, he'd fashion a gun out of wood
and take aim at the world 'round his room.
My brother, a juggler with the show,
told me years ago he considered the boy off
somewhere in his own universe
where a glum face tells the world to stay away.
I don't know about these things, but he's gone."

The crowds dissolve by evening,
and the animals relax in their cages and stalls;
the chimps clean each other;
the amazing oversized tarantula—
accustomed to spinning her horrible webs
just feet above the children—
is boxed up for the night. Strings of light
play all along the sawdust pathways
while the barker bows his head, unsmiling,
bereft of love that grows old in hiding.

Daily Grief

the dripping sounds
and a sudden draft:

it's raining again
amidst the ding dong clouds
smudged above this posted house
made of chinks and thin armor.

> *sad are the hours since he's gone*
> *too far to catch and play;*

some damp has crept inside
and the one closet no longer opens;
this wet intrusion approaches
a coverless grief:

muscles tighten against the botched chances;
thus the creep to lassitude;
cramps too cold to unknot—
lamentation beyond the rules

> *…the hours since he's gone*
> *too far to catch and play;*

the heart too—
suffers the rain's invasion—
behaves wildly & holds no promise,
no spell of relief

> *…since he's gone*
> *too far to catch and play.*

Touch

is a gift for hunger
as well as for loneliness,
a wafer pure and secular.
Loam crawls with life,
clean as the wish
to send innocent arms
around innocent shoulders.
Arms or shoulders
are any way candid and pure.

Harbinger of union:
the enduring condition
of a well-practiced heart.

4. Jazz

Listening

I hear the distant laughter from childish voices
behind the bushes maybe—
no seeing, no telling from here.

I hear a distant conversation, a contention
on topics too faint to follow or dream up.

I hear the distant drums from ancient days to now,
these in-your-face this time tom-tom drums.

I hear the far-off cries of birds flying circles
some dropping down; some flying higher.

I hear the whispers of delight and defiance
twist to a whole new sound.

I hear cow bells proclaiming evidence of cow;
I hear the train whistle's demonstration.

I hear the cat calls of reason and unreason
above the hosannas of PLEASE LET US BE

[off the rhythm]

played on tenor sax at an outdoors club
just yards from the beach

and the silent moon above the beach
is half-hidden by clouds
and everyone's wandering attention.

Phone Calls to Make

Call the butcher
to deliver beefsteak
many pounds prime
call the lemonade
call the editor—take my silver
take my gold
call the gunsmith
powder the muzzle
call the meter-reader
must have been drunk bleary-eyed
or criminal
call the priest of the seven veils
a kiss the phone goodbye
call the lemonade
call the one who baits your heart
call the angels from out the dark
whispering low
call the lemonade
call the cobbler to do his best
call the doctor
the machine says—call back after
call the lemonade
call the weatherman
call the enemy where he rests
where he plots where he mourns
bring him 'round—debts cancelled
safe passage promised and delivered
call the lemonade
call the children
call the children
of those who called before

Bigs and Littles

a wee little breeze
a big buzz in someone's bonnet

a bigger blast in the yard
little porcelains all in pieces

big noise over the news
that the littlest gene sparked a theory
a big deal
and the little he cares
big sky
little children
big living room
little time to spend

and the earth makes its rounds
a big orbit around the sun:
little earth
little most everything

Backstage

I've seen the backstage flowers
held in the grip of luck.
I've seen the hold slip and
the flowers fall
into the hall's dark corners,
delicate colors caught
in the floorboards' grain.

Backstage, waiting to go on,
you envision flowers handed over
modestly or as a taunt, a jibe,
a jinx to give you courage
before you sing or dance or speechify
the night away;
the dark corners invite your return.

The stained grain of the floorboards
can't feel your feet at all—as they fall
lightly after triumph or leadenly
after some lapse in delivery.
Yet, season after season,
flowers arrive in profusion
filling the backstage areas,
their extravagance absorbed in fragrance,
even as the floor invites these bouquets,
fragile as a night ago.

Blue Smoke Above the Bandstand at Fat Tuesdays

Watching her that way,
with the music skipping,
was a pleasure worth the trip downtown
and later, the one back home as well.

But why did she want me watching?
The invitation was for that
and for Billy Higgins: who could resist
Higgins & Co. and there,
along with memory,
the shape of my old flame.

Maybe in those days
she enjoyed the feel of my 20-foot gaze,
and even, sometimes, my hovering,
tapping the keys ever after.

The quintet burned
as I did on a different wick,
sitting at the bar near the door
30 feet from the stage
while right up front
in a cluster of jittery joy,
sat this old flame smoking
in the company of a new flame
leaning in her direction.

Blue smoke rose
from the hands and mouths
at her table, wafted across
and butted up against the low ceiling
which held it, sequestered it, puffing
with each ratchet of sound.

Cedar Walton's riffs,
joyous in three speeds,
blasted and whispered
wild freedom within a perfect frame.

We too had been wanton
but couldn't do more than improvise—
she with her surges, her aerial leaps,
me with my bellows and holdouts.

We should have borrowed the music's frame.
As it was, we made it up
as it came and went
from spellbound to spellbinder.

Blues Again

Lying in bed, waiting for sleep
or something entirely different
to come up,
I heard a whimper in the tick tock blue
and dipped into the distance, sky blue
and far from this room with its eight-bar blues
and the tick tock again of the clock
with your voice going out the door.

The weight of these sounds still bears
the color of water under a blue dome
and I am alone with a twelve-bar blues,
love having fled its comfort;

lying in bed now, sweating blue bullets
a paintball splatter to the skull—
my eyes closed, my ears dimmed;
the keenness of sleep is yards away
blinking, darting fitfully into a blue day.

Postmodernism

Zero winks—easing around the corner,
his black brim showing,
fire falling about his shoulders
burning close before cooling.
He survives every time.
He's a paid fist
on somebody's side.

If you think Zero's bad
check out Minus,
the post-modern freak,
reclining, a claw beckoning,
the middle digit on his right hand
curling, little spasmodic scratchings
in the air.

Minus is colder than ever.
Look in his mouth.
If Zero is modern,
this monster is post.

Petulance

Call him Tommy the actor
glum when no one's looking
petulant and restive
lips pursed and slit red
his eyes too red around
the peering browns
he pauses to weigh his effect
writes nothing down for a long while
he scowls
then he writes spleen.

He knows the condition
was ticked off on the brink of joy
been there among the black looks
the fouled ditches
a jewel nearby slips under something
the offending faces
turned around
he feels they are beautiful and
knows they are fluent in languages.

Tommy—a fellow glowering in high dudgeon—
sideways a crab
and all along shaking his head no
and no again as if one day
this shaking might distract someone
outside himself.

Portrait

Mr. Stealth, oiling around the corner,
is jiggling the pennies
plucked from the eyes of the dead.
Is he gothic?
No, he simply has hands that won't stay still,
twitchy hands in the isles of the dead.

He'll steal the shadow from under a rented chair
and he's quiet as a stifled breath;
fold what he says in a blade of grass.
He'll snatch a tune out of the air,
hum it sideways,
and leave the bird another.

Tireless in his wanderings abroad,
he pries open the secrets of the dead
and watches their days wind backwards.
But sometimes he stays home
imagining the faith of those 12 tribes
famous for their wanderings.

Once he started moving out a little
he discovered stealth.

Jack the Hat

One of the sorriest individuals
to ever scrape leather on Joy St.,
was a man named Jack the Hat,

"one of the hippest cats
on the hang-out scene
many yards of silver ago,"

a fellow loiterer once said; but
the truth, as always, was different:
he had long-range eyes,

looking over into the next town
or valley all the time
fancying himself a sneak-thief.

Most times, dedicated to a whim away,
he was scarcely near
where ever he was.

Finally they branded him a bad actor,
shortened his performances, then
zap! the curtain came down.

A Bunch of Could Haves

you misunderstood
I said lust not last
I said suck not dust
I said now not before

you misunderstood
looked up when you could have seen me
looked down when you should have seen her
looked sad when joy was a yard away

you misunderstood even after
and could have come home though late
and grown to tolerate a cutting edge
banked in gentle humor
and could have fathomed
and grown part of
this house of good cards.

Drinking

When presented a shot of whisky,
single malt and easy down,
I tip back
and tip back twice
and tell the tender bend his elbow
and on his way erase the frown.

Conversation floats on another night
and it's gin this time and just as fine
surrounding an ice, ready as sin;
double the dose for kindness
with a leaf of mint, drop of lime—
and the barmaid's smile is lovely.

Pastis is a tasty glide, Pernod too
at home and in the public spaces:
half of this and half of water
and it seems the healthiest kind of gesture.
That's just my tastes: an old man
dolled up and speaking like a boy.

Late at night it's Cognac dear
and I say dear alone and in company.
Wisdom—well—you're dead if you do
and equally deep if you don't,
so I sip my libations eternal.
After all I've taken in and more,

I'm begging you, old Reaper,
when you show up in your hood,
you thief in the form of a shadow,
leave the lectures home,
let me empty the glass
and your stroke be swift and clean.

Under the Spell of Muggles

The spark of a thought dies
in the Lethe-like chambers of the brain's frail skull.
Peek around for it & the precious iota goes scurrying
beneath some fold, rimple, or nano-speck
of myelin covering.

Right now, under the muggles,
I know right from left,
and how to talk cozily to cats,
but the center of the sentence knows not
its origin or where it's tracking.

OK, forget it; I'll rest back in the liquid element,
bathe medium warm & doze.
There's a magazine on the shelf
lying across the tub and freshly rolled spliffs.
I'll enjoy the off-color prints, and then—
the deep suck of the Viper.

In the Parlance of Mezz

after Mezz Mezzrow

As Mezz used to say when tired—
after playing too excitedly for hours
and after hours and then topping it off
with too much good down brew, muggles too—
it's time "to stash my frame
between a deuce of lilywhites,"
and if that hurts the rhythm of my day
or alters the moves of some,
that's OK; after all, days do have their jaggeds.

"Plant you now and dig you later,"
is a farewell in spades I've said
and no offense;
I was born in the light of a stairwell
and have always been color-blind
or partial to black velvet day or night.
That's just my mind.

For some—me too for a patch of years—
it's been Weep City just around every turn
and the conveyance an express.
I'm off it now and sit miles from the station.
My misery's been gone for more than
a couple of chimes and I'm up sometimes
and playing quicker than a spinning dime.

I've known meanness too and stridency
and blades in the hands of tigers
hiding their purrs within.
I said one time to a cat with a permanent frown,
"You can afford the luxury of being a little delicate,
my friend." Fur bristled—gained his face a grin.

After all the times inside cells and cellblocks
and blocked in my own self too, I'm out and
in the music again. Pops is my guiding star
and it's all for the telling:
I'm a "skin full of contentment,
a bundle of happiness in a blue serge suit."

A Man in Trousers

Who is he
slowly walking into his reputation,
and then when his pace quickens
he stumbles gracefully
and rights himself—
a hunter, a warrior
some special person who'd give up
his blade and a large slice of time
to negotiate a peace between nations?

He plays a wicked game of chess.

His eyes are bloodshot
His mouth is grinning
His ears hear nothing
His eyes are bloodshot
as he says.

He writes profusely in his journal.

Who was he
before the chute sailed him down
to safety so many years ago?
No one remembers.

Is he a believer or not?
Someone who cheats at cards
or not?
A kind bastard—as the expression goes,
or is it all misunderstanding
given the conditions sighted in the latest bulletins?
He's a man with pockets,
sometimes full and flush,
sometimes as empty as drugged sleep.

Who is he?
Well, he's something in trousers.

Blues 1

You
catch my breath with your waking

a calf moves closer to its mother
slumbering

some brother leaves his home
to bring me what I need.
It doesn't work & I call you back

Sugar—I call you Sugar

no rest in my slumber
no sugar in my bowl

Blues 2

Such accidents do happen
dancing: she says
I'm dancing beneath your loving blow
so I stagger

staggered, he says no:
it wasn't a blow
it was a brush—feather light;
I fly round the world for your gold

another time
she tries so hard
to make him well,
it makes her sleepy.

more lately
they share their tricks
but never their secrets
set in codes, dark and changing.
They can barely read what they say,
and when they do, they forget.

The Mafia Was on Strike; Go Ask Pacos

Pacos darling,
what are you doing in my beans?

Or where will you go in the twilight
before the fair?

The questions hang on the murder tree;
the leaves challenge fear.

Pacos, your place on the trigger wish
is the committee's strength;

we've known this
for three safe but dull years.

Where might we go tomorrow
and to whose crib when someone's out?

The fair needs your swift arrival
for the needed, long-awaited shift.

With no sunlight in prospect,
what will you plant there, Pacos?

Should we run to our lawyers
or join the law in a bust?

Rabbits on Castle Grounds

The place is mad with rabbits.
Far more are bought than sold.
The man is tied to his habits.

They clog up all the turrets,
Have trysts in every fold.
The place is mad with rabbits.

Strewn everywhere like addicts
One's bound to feed and hold,
The man is tied to his habits.

For years, his friends, the Cabots,
Have said: "Go see. Behold.
The place is mad with rabbits

All chasing tails to grab bits
Of flaunted fluff—they're bold."
The man is tied to his habits.

He studies all their antics.
He treats them like they're gold.
The place is mad with rabbits.
The man is tied to his habits.

Barry Wallenstein was born in New York City. He received his PhD in modern poetry from New York University in 1972. Early poems first appeared in 1964 and since then six collections of poetry have been published. In the early 1970s he began collaborating with jazz artists in the performance and recording of his poetry, and he continues to perform with musicians internationally. From 1965 until 2006 he taught literature and writing at the City College of New York where he founded The Poetry Outreach Center, in which he continues to be involved as Professor Emeritus. He currently resides with his wife, Lorna, on Riverside Drive close to where he lived as a child. He lives part of each year in an old log house in the Catskills.

About NYQ Books™

NYQ Books™ was established in 2009 as an imprint of The New York Quarterly Foundation, Inc. Its mission is to augment the *New York Quarterly* poetry magazine by providing an additional venue for poets already published in the magazine. A lifelong dream of NYQ's founding editor, William Packard, NYQ Books™ has been made possible by both growing foundation support and new technology that was not available during William Packard's lifetime. We are proud to present these books to you and hope that you will continue to support The New York Quarterly Foundation, Inc. and our poets and that you will enjoy these other titles from NYQ Books™:

Barbara Blatner	*The Still Position*
Amanda J. Bradley	*Hints and Allegations*
rd coleman	*beach tracks*
Joanna Crispi	*Soldier in the Grass*
Ira Joe Fisher	*Songs from an Earlier Century*
Sanford Fraser	*Tourist*
Tony Gloeggler	*The Last Lie*
Ted Jonathan	*Bones & Jokes*
Richard Kostelanetz	*Recircuits*
Iris Lee	*Urban Bird Life*
Kevin Pilkington	*In the Eyes of a Dog*
Jim Reese	*ghost on 3rd*
F. D. Reeve	*The Puzzle Master and Other Poems*
Jackie Sheeler	*Earthquake Came to Harlem*
Jayne Lyn Stahl	*Riding with Destiny*
Shelley Stenhouse	*Impunity*
Tim Suermondt	*Just Beautiful*
Douglas Treem	*Everything so Seriously*
Oren Wagner	*Voluptuous Gloom*
Joe Weil	*The Plumber's Apprentice*
Pui Ying Wong	*Yellow Plum Season*
Fred Yannantuono	*A Boilermaker for the Lady*
Grace Zabriskie	*Poems*

Please visit our website for these and other titles:
www.nyqbooks.org